Praise for *Ch...*

'An inspiring manual that gives tangible and holistic guidance on how to lead during the very messy times we're living in.' KAJAL ODEDRA, GLOBAL COMMUNICATIONS DIRECTOR, CHANGE.ORG AND AUTHOR, DO SOMETHING: ACTIVISM FOR EVERYONE

'Katy Murray equips us with tools to deepen our self-awareness and hold ourselves accountable. Katy provides the support to discover our purpose, keep swinging a pickaxe at our disruptive spot in the wall of systemic inequality, and chip away with our change-making power.' ANNE FOSTER, DIRECTOR OF DIVERSITY AND INCLUSION

'This book should be in every aspiring change maker's toolkit! Katy Murray lays out practical steps on both the inner and outer work of change. A must-read!' JENNIFER BROWN, FOUNDER AND CEO, JENNIFER BROWN CONSULTING, AUTHOR, INCLUSION: DIVERSITY, THE NEW WORKPLACE & THE WILL TO CHANGE AND PODCASTER, THE WILL TO CHANGE

'This book spoke to my soul. I always struggle with the expectations of "doing it all" and "always being on" that come with the "change maker" label. Katy Murray's book is the perfect salve and antidote to toxic productivity. A revelation.' COLLETTE PHILIP, FOUNDER AND MANAGING DIRECTOR, BRAND BY ME

'Katy Murray's book provides the understanding and practical tools and techniques to grow and support others' growth at work, while also preserving (and cherishing) space for yourself. It's a thoughtful and thought-provoking book – like a personal leadership coach in your pocket – allowing you to dip in, or dip back, when you need it.' LOTTE SPENCER, GLOBAL DIRECTOR OF CONSUMER PRODUCT MARKETING, SPOTIFY

'Every aspiring change maker needs this book! It teaches you practically how to build resilience, home in on your purpose and make a difference in your world. Katy Murray makes these often-woolly topics concrete and actionable with examples, exercises and reflection prompts. All written in her unmistakable voice – encouraging and nerve-giving – and above all kind.' FIONA YOUNG, HEAD OF PROGRAMS AND DIVERSITY, EQUITY & INCLUSION PRACTICE LEAD, HIVE LEARNING

'For all of us that have had those days where we wonder why we are tired, why we do what we do, why we even bother to keep trying to achieve – this book can help. Katy Murray guides us to recognize our own individual power, how to own it and how to use it in a sustainable way.' LIDIA OSHLYANSKY, CHIEF PRODUCT OFFICER, BOUGHT BY MANY/MANY PETS

'*Change Makers* is the manual for any woman. Not afraid to challenge readers with questions all women should face as they grow and develop, it celebrates femininity and showcases women who are changing our future. This book is a must for all my mentees!' JESSICA HARVEY, FOUNDER, THE FEMALE MENTORING ALLIANCE, MANAGING DIRECTOR AND CHIEF CONTROL OFFICER IN THE FINANCE INDUSTRY

Change Makers

A woman's guide to stepping up without burning out at work

Katy Murray

KoganPage

Publisher's note

Every possible effort has been made to ensure that the information contained in this book is accurate at the time of going to press, and the publishers and author cannot accept responsibility for any errors or omissions, however caused. No responsibility for loss or damage occasioned to any person acting, or refraining from action, as a result of the material in this publication can be accepted by the editor, the publisher or the author.

First published in Great Britain and the United States in 2022 by Kogan Page Limited

2nd Floor, 45 Gee Street	8 W 38th Street, Suite 902	4737/23 Ansari Road
London	New York, NY 10018	Daryaganj
EC1V 3RS	USA	New Delhi 110002
United Kingdom		India
www.koganpage.com		

Kogan Page books are printed on paper from sustainable forests.

ISBNs

Hardback	978 1 3986 0508 4
Paperback	978 1 3986 0506 0
Ebook	978 1 3986 0507 7

British Library Cataloguing-in-Publication Data

A CIP record for this book is available from the British Library.

Library of Congress Cataloging-in-Publication Data

Names: Murray, Katy, author.
Title: Change makers : a woman's guide to stepping up without burning out at work / Katy Murray.
Description: London, United Kingdom ; New York, NY : Kogan Page Limited, 2022. | Includes bibliographical references and index.
Identifiers: LCCN 2021062031 (print) | LCCN 2021062032 (ebook) | ISBN 9781398605060 (paperback) | ISBN 9781398605084 (hardback) | ISBN 9781398605077 (ebook)
Subjects: LCSH: Women–Vocational guidance. | Burn out (Psychology) | Businesswomen. | Success in business.
Classification: LCC HF5382.6 .M87 2022 (print) | LCC HF5382.6 (ebook) | DDC 650.1082–dc23/eng/20220228
LC record available at https://lccn.loc.gov/2021062031
LC ebook record available at https://lccn.loc.gov/2021062032

Typeset by Integra Software Services, Pondicherry
Print production managed by Jellyfish
Printed and bound by CPI Group (UK) Ltd, Croydon, CR0 4YY

For E and N

Contents

List of figures and tables

About the author

Katy Murray is a leadership development coach, consultant, facilitator and speaker. She's coached thousands of leaders over 25 years and hosted workshops and conferences in 35 countries across the world. Named one of the Top 50 UK D&I leaders to follow, Katy is the Director of Catalyst Collective, a boutique inclusion consultancy, equipping organizations to co-create more equitable workplaces. She lives in the Lake District, UK.

About this book

Change Makers is designed to power you up in all kinds of ways.

Drawing wisdom and insight from spirituality, performance coaching, inclusion and intersectional feminism, Katy invites you on a journey of self-discovery and systems awareness, so that you can step up in your change-making leadership, without burning out!

Acknowledgements

I m so grateful to all my clients, colleagues, collaborators and co-conspirators, shaping my thinking and practice over two decades.

Check out the bonus resources at my site www.katy catalyst.com/change-makers-book, including a themed bibliography.

Thank you for:

What you put out into the world: Rob Bell, Sarah Bessey, adrienne maree brown, Austin Channing, Cristena Cleveland, Emma Dabiri, Glennon Doyle, Morgan Harper Nichols, Blair Imani, Francesca Leigh, Natalia Nana Lester Bush, Nova Reid, Jo Saxton.

Programmes, supervision, coaching, business development, guided reflection and study with Desiree Adaway, Eleanor Beaton, Rachel Cargle, Revd Dr Kate Coleman, Jessica Fish, Marie Forleo, Ericka Hines, Tara Mohr, Kate Northrup, Leesa Renee Hall, Layla Saad, Lucy Sheridan.

Workshop design, facilitation and learning alongside Seamus Anderson, Antonio Belgrave, Vanessa Belleau, Upasna Bhadhal, Will Campbell, Ali Carruthers, Judy Castano, Louise Coningsby, Kev Cottee-Wort, Bill Crooks, Carl Davies, Emma Dipper, Ben Evans, Sarah Fraser, Rob Funning, Liz Goold, Nancy Hinga, Rick James, Sheila Jones, Satwant Kaur, Rob Kelly, Richard Marshall, Betsy Mboizi, Mary Musselbrook, Roianne Nedd, William Ogara, Lotta Ranefall, Jo Royle, Roberto Santiago, Fiona Smith, Carol Tavernier, Nikunj Upadhyay, Nick Wright.

Walk 'n' talks and soul-stretching conversations with Cat Blyth, Ali Carruthers, Sophie Clarke, Fi Cuthill, Joshua Karl, Di Murray, Jennifer Ogunyemi, Collette Philip Keen, Jenny Ross, Kate Simpson, Liz Ward.

I'm grateful to each of my brilliant clients.

I invited clients, subscribers and wider members of my community to share their perspectives on the themes in this book. The compassionate humanity, raw vulnerability, playfulness and depth of wisdom made me laugh and cry and my heart expand. You raised the bar for what I wanted to write for you. In addition to those named above, thank you Ayo Abbas, Jaz Broughton, Emily Button, Jacqueline Conway, Caroline Ellis, Julie Fedele, Donna Ford, Alison Glasspool, Ros Holland, Ruth Holmes, Keri Jarvis, Anthea Lawson, Caroline Leigh, Melisa Lindros, Ranee Long, Tommy Ludgate, Alison Marshall, Mandy Marshall, Steph Mary, Dr Rebecca Kate Maudling, Victoria Smith Murphy, Aarti Palmer, Jess Ratcliffe, Cathy Reay, Jo Richardson, Becky Vicars, Holly Whelan, Rebecca Whinfrey, Fiona Young.

For all that you role model and your inspiring change-maker interviews, thank you Keiko Asano, Sonya Barlow, Lauren Currie, Naomi Evans, Mireille Harper, Leyla Hussein, Khaleelah Jones, Alice Olins, Lara Sheldrake, Tamu Thomas, Davinia Tomlinson.

Also big thanks to:

Charlotte Jenkins, Alison Jones and Lucy Werner for early guidance in getting this book past the ideas stage.

Géraldine Collard and Kogan Page for building this book! Sakina Saidi for the collaboration and your brilliant Intersectionality Map.

Edie Murray for your annotations.

Sara Dalrymple for the Shoreditch granola stop as we captured headshots.

Lori and Richard for pro tips on how to write and structure a manuscript.

Yard 46, Brew Brothers and Waterside cafes for copious peppermint tea and Cat for yoga balm.

Ann and Wattie, I appreciate you hosting my writing retreats.

Kate for the long-distance running analogies.

Beren for holding kind, expansive space.

Nair and my team for filling the gaps.

Finally…

Angus, you're the bass note.

Edie and Norah, this book is dedicated to you.

Introduction

If you've come here to help me, you're wasting your time. But if you've come because your liberation is bound up with mine, then let us work together. LILLA WATSON[1]

Welcome, Change Maker!

There's a forest that's guarded by a huge tower. At the top of the tower sits a sentry, sipping her tea and looking out for passers-by. She has two questions she asks all-comers and she waits, poised and ready to call out in her loudest voice.

One day a woman sets out on a journey, seeking adventure. She sees the tower in the distance, behind it the dense forest. She approaches with trepidation, also curiosity. She's heard there's a sentry who sits in the tower, waiting to share her wisdom with every passer-by.

As she walks closer, she sees the sentry jump to her feet, sploshing her tea.

The questions ring out:

'Who are you?'
'Why are you here?'

The woman stops. She sits down.

'How much do you get paid to sit up there and call out those questions to every passer-by?' she asks the sentry.

The sentry gives the sum.

'Let me pay you three times that amount, if you'll come find me every morning, to ask me those two very questions.'

These powerful questions, 'who am I?' and 'why am I here?', are at the heart of this book. In my day-to-day work coaching change-making women, I notice the questions bubble under the surface of every conversation.

If you've picked up this book, you're probably exploring these questions too. Welcome!

You may be experiencing the expectations, the overwhelm, the burnout, that's perpetuated in our workplaces and organizational systems. We're leading in the context of unprecedented uncertainty and we're choosing how to respond in such tumultuous times. You've become more aware of systemic oppression, injustice, societal inequities, and you're desiring change. Maybe this is a new emerging consciousness – a call to justice and fairness in society and equity in our workplaces that you've not previously needed or wanted to engage with, due to your own privilege. Maybe this is an awareness you've held a while, or part of your lived experience, and now joining a wider consciousness. You're aware of the climate emergency and the need to engage.[2]

We're experiencing an individual and growing collective sense of 'this is not working anymore'. Maybe you've felt it, or you're feeling it right now, too?

We don't want to keep propping up systems that aren't working. We want to be part of what's emerging.

There's a new world of work emerging and it's infinitely kinder, more balanced, reflective of all the range of people in our society. This will benefit *everyone*.[3]

You're drawn to the idea of being a 'change maker' but the words sound weighty – is that really me? Can I really make a difference?

So, what makes a change maker? A change maker is someone who sees how current workplaces and systems hold them and others back. If you're a change maker you'll want to overcome that and co-create something better. You're passionate about issues, causes, challenges in the world around you, and you want to feel like you're making a difference. You want to find more purpose in your life and work *and* you want to be part of creating more equitable workspaces. You know this work is messy, hard, complex, and you need to maximize your resilience along the way. You understand that the two questions the sentry asks are at the centre of finding *your* change-making power.

The wall and finding our part to play

Our cultural conditioning runs deep – it includes norms, expectations, ways of working, and behaviours that shape us and our beliefs about what's possible for our lives, our workplaces, and the world around us. The interconnected web of capitalism, patriarchy, ableism and white supremacy (and all the other -isms and -archies) can keep us trapped, compliant and believing we're not powerful enough to make a difference. We have to be vigilant to keep noticing, then unpacking and unlearning how these factors shape us.

As change makers, we can imagine systems of patriarchy, misogyny, racism, ableism, heteronormativity – systemic oppression – as interconnected bricks, making up a huge wall. It's solid, it's large, it's oppressive. It's too much for just one person to scale this wall, or to bring it down on their own. Instead, we can imagine that we each take a pickaxe and choose our place at the wall, where we can slowly start to pick away at it. Over time, with consistent picking, the wall will come down.[4] This book will help you to see the wall, spot your place at it, and give you the tools to start picking away at it.

REFLECTION POINT

Are you standing at the wall yet?

Have you found your place? Are you new to the wall and wondering where to start?

Are you looking for where you can best contribute?

Have you been here a while and getting tired now, needing some refreshment?

....

....

....

....

....

So, this book is not to 'rescue' you; you are not broken!

This book invites you to find your part to play, to ask what is *my* contribution going to be?

In your workplace context, in your career, which is the piece of the wall you're chipping away at? How are you going to be part of dismantling systems?

It's more than you...

I'm passionate about you stepping up into your full potential, living on purpose and doing this in a sustainable way. But this is not an individual journey, you climbing the ladder and 'winning' at an old system, at the expense of others. This is not about you playing the game that's not been designed or created for you. As Kelly Diels encourages us, 'we can act back against the systems that are limiting us, rather than just seeking to do a little bit better individually within that system'.

And more than this. As Lilla Watson reminds us, 'my liberation is connected to yours'. It's not enough that I create a great life for just me. There's a narrative, to which white women (supported and encouraged historically by white feminism) are particularly susceptible, that the best we can hope for, what we should aim for, is to navigate our way and find ways to fit into workplace systems and gain what benefit we can. It's like giving a lick of paint to an old system so it's 'less bad'. I'm not interested in that.

I'm passionate about systems and structures that work for everyone. So, this book is also about being part of co-creating new systems that embed justice and wellbeing for all. Part of that will be about seeing how we (where we hold privilege) have been protected by, and have perpetuated, those systems.

Businesses are 'waking up', they're changing, they're seeing they need to be part of the change, on the 'right side of history'.

I want to be part of this revolution, do you?

I don't fully know, and it's not yet fully clear, what this new world of work (and other spaces in society) will look like. It's emerging. We'll need to be actively dismantling and re-creating systems. We can all choose to be part of this work, in whatever way it feels good and is sustainable for us, and whatever our spheres of influence.

Sustaining our change making

McKinsey report that 42 per cent of women said they 'often' or 'almost always' experienced burn out in 2021 compared with 32 per cent a year ago, and that one in three considered leaving the workforce or downshifting their careers.[5] Deloitte is reporting this as 23 per cent.[6] Over half (53%) of women say their mental health suffers to the point of burnout because of their jobs, all or some of the time.[7]

We need to sustain our resilience and wellbeing in this work as change makers! When we're engaging with change, whether it's in our communities or workplaces, it takes energy. Burnout is rife among change-making leaders, and particularly among marginalized groups, due to the energy required to navigate workplaces.[8]

We need to value our self-care and our own sustainability. Burnout for the sake of a cause we're passionate about, or in response to workplace pressures, is very common, but not inevitable, nor should it be expected. This book invites you to consider the role of hope, joy, self-compassion and pleasure as essential and integral pieces of your change making and day-to-day leadership. The power practices in this book will support you to step up without burning out!

A note about intersectionality, privilege and the importance of multiple stories

All are welcome here. I'm centring women's and non-binary folks' experiences in this book. The notion of the 'default' in our society, which I mentioned above, means that most business and leadership books are written by and centre on a male, heterosexual, cis-gendered, able-bodied, neurotypical, Caucasian perspective.

My desire and aim in this book is to open up new perspectives, reflect a wider lived experience and be part of revealing bias, prejudice, privilege and how it plays out and perpetuates systemic injustice. As Maya Angelou is widely reported to have said, 'when you know better, do better'.

In choosing contributors I've been thoughtful about a range of perspectives. Listening to multiple stories opens up our 'echo chambers' (perpetuated by the algorithms of social media) and is a way for us to deepen our awareness and minimize our own biases. But my contributors are speaking for themselves; they don't represent a wider group or issue, and not all possible perspectives are represented here. There are further stories and resources on my site (www.katycatalyst.com/change-makers-book) to enable you to widen your perspectives.

The pioneers, movers and shakers who've contributed their voices to this book are the change-making women I'm learning from and inspired by, and you'll hear their insights throughout the book. Women who've found their own path, creating 'new tables', disrupting and challenging the status quo, from inside workplaces and organizations, and from the outside. In addition, 30 women contributed their perspectives to a questionnaire during Summer 2021. These women come from the worlds of business, design, education, engineering, entrepreneurship, financial services, health care, humanitarian work, politics, social impact and tech. When I see each of these women chipping away at their part of the wall, it inspires me to keep chipping away at my part!

In desiring to take this intersectional perspective, I'm aware of how my own identity shows up. As a white, able-bodied, cis-gendered, heterosexual and neurotypical woman, I hold significant privilege in my body and identity, in addition to education and wealth privilege from my background. I'll talk about the topics in this book imperfectly. I'll have my own blind spots. I'm choosing to show up imperfectly and willing to learn, rather than not at all. I love how change-maker Leyla Hussein puts this: 'I'm forever a student. People say "I'm happily ever after" and I'm "happily ever in progress" – that's me, I'm ok with that!' (you'll hear more from Leyla in Chapter 3).

The purpose of this book is to resource you as an individual and equip you to navigate and co-create the systems you're in.

> I have a hard time with the word 'resilience'. I don't think it's a coincidence that being a 'resilient woman' has become very trendy at the same time inequality is rising and women are being disproportionately affected by austerity policies. I want us to expose and challenge the social structures causing women to be in crisis – instead of putting all the onus on women to learn to be resilient. (Lauren Currie)

There's *inner work*, and there's *outer* work.

The *inner work* is about tuning into your desires, honouring your body's needs, centring your wellbeing, overcoming internal resistance, building your self-efficacy, sustaining yourself to stand in your own agency and power, so that you can step up in your leadership.

The *outer work* enables you to navigate the systems you find yourself in, be part of chipping away at the wall, re-creating the old systems and co-creating something new.

This book explores and equips you for both, so you can step up without burning out! We start with you and build out from there.

We need to do the work as individuals, but we also need to work collectively. We can't solve world and workplace issues of inequality through personal development alone. This book invites you to consider who you can align with, support and engage along the way. (Hot tip! This makes it more fun, effective and sustainable, promise!)

All models are wrong, some are useful[9]

Throughout this book, I'm sharing models, frameworks, themes, ideas and perspectives from a wide range of disciplines and thinkers. I draw my learning from ancient wisdom traditions, spirituality, personal development, leadership and organization development, social and behavioural psychology, therapeutic practices and performance coaching, as well as intersectional feminism, womanism, organizational performance, diversity, equity, inclusion and anti-racism. These have been gleaned and gathered through my 20+ years of practice as an organizational development consultant, facilitator, coach, business leader and human attempting to live a good life! I'm so grateful to all my clients, colleagues and collaborators over the years, where we've tested and refined these approaches.

No one model will tell the full story, or have the full perspective. If you're looking for a set answer or the ABC formula, you may feel frustrated here! None of the models or ideas is the 'only one' that solves everything, explains everything, nor all you need to navigate through life. They're each perspectives and insights that I've found useful, and I'm sharing different approaches to guide you through your own exploration of these topics, much as I would if we were coaching together one-to-one.

The map is not the territory[10] and these are just maps, not the territory, of your unique, complex, precious life. You can think of them as layers that build up a collage, or different lenses through which to look.

You are a change maker!

These are the **key principles** that underpin my coaching approach and practice, and form the foundational beliefs I have about *you,* as you read this book:

1 You and your life are innately valuable.
2 You are powerful.
3 Life is precious.
4 You are not broken; you don't need to be fixed.
5 Your quest for purpose and meaning in your life and work is valid.
6 Your resilience and wellbeing are paramount.
7 You are a change maker!

Let's take each by turn.

1 **You and your life are innately valuable.** There's only one of you. You've a unique mix of strengths, gifts, perspectives and life experiences. You're valuable as a human *being,* whatever you choose to *do,* or *not do.* We're socialized to believe that we *should* be x, y or z, or that we need more of a, b or c to be worthy and successful. But you are enough. Just as you are. Your life has brilliance, meaning and potential just by *being.* Use this book to help you tune into your own purpose, joy and validation of who you uniquely are.

2 **You are powerful.** You have power and agency. I believe you can find and use your power, whatever your start-point. You maybe don't always feel like a leader, let alone a change maker. This book will help you tune into and activate your power.

However, I don't believe that we individually create *all* of our reality. Let's acknowledge that systems of oppression affect us (most specifically if you hold an aspect of your identity that's marginalized). Life circumstances, which you didn't personally create, affect you and your life. Systemic injustice that you don't control may be affecting you and your life. This book will help you notice, name and navigate that, as well as be part of interrupting, disrupting and dismantling those systems.

3 **Life is precious.** My mum died aged 43, and one of the key lessons (among many) seared into my consciousness through that loss is that each human life is precious and, often, short. We can wait to build a legacy, we can live with a sense of 'I'll do that *when...*' or 'I'll get to that *if...*'. We can end up putting things off, with a sense of what we might want to do, or who we might want to be, sometime in the future. I've learned that we actually only have the present moment, recurring again and again, the eternal now.[11] The invitation is to *be in the present moment*, to squeeze the goodness out of each day, to live life fully and abundantly. Use this book to help you get clear on the life that you want to create for yourself.

4 **You are not broken; you don't need to be fixed.** We live in a world, and work in workplaces, designed by and for a default identity,[12] which suits those who're part of that dominant identity. We're socialized to believe that we need to be *fixed*, in order to participate. Society projects unobtainable goals and teaches us to beat ourselves up when we don't or can't achieve them. If we do achieve them, there's always another unobtainable

goal on the horizon. I'm not thin enough, pretty enough, tall/young/old/clever/fill-in-the-blank   enough!   This quest for enoughness is never-ending and self-perpetuating. If you hold aspects of your identity which are marginalized, this may be exacerbated even more. I don't believe that you and I are not enough. I see this as a lie; it's the system that's not designed for our fullest flourishing. I do believe we can learn to navigate these spaces and workplaces. I also believe we can be part of collective action to change oppressive systems that negatively impact the lives of others, and be part of co-creating new systems. Use this book to help you do that!

5 **Your quest for purpose and meaning in your life and work is valid.** Your current work and career trajectory may provide that sense of fulfilment and adventure for you – great! Use this book to help you deepen your resilience and dial up your change-making impact. You may be finding that your current work and career is *not* providing that vitality for you and if so – great! Use this book to help you reconnect with your own sense of purpose and realign your choices, so you can create more of the life you most want to live and make the contribution you want to be making. Stay curious!

6 **Your resilience and wellbeing are paramount.** I'm not here for the toxic narrative which prioritizes your wellbeing so that you can be more productive and more able to participate in the capitalist systems that dominate our society. As change makers we're not immune to this thinking; over-drive and burnout are common. Your wellbeing is valid in and of itself. Your health and wellness are key to your functioning and flourishing as a human

and you can build your resilience. Honouring your needs, your desires, your body, your joy and pleasure, your sustainability is *part of* your change making. You're not any less valuable if you aren't healthy or fit. We also know that trauma, including generational trauma, is stored and experienced in our bodies.[13] There are times in life when we do feel broken, when we experience grief, distress, burnout, as part of the experience of being human. Seeking healing, help and support is an essential part of your flourishing as a human. Use this book to help you validate and prioritize your own wellbeing in your day-to-day life and change-making leadership.

7 **You are a change maker!** Each of us can influence those around us, each of us can have a positive impact on our workplaces and on our planet. Notice the desires inside you, the spaces in you that want to lead, that want to step up, speak out and make a difference. The parts of you that are angry, curious, devastated by the injustices you see. The parts of you that are energized and excited by the opportunities for change. Not sure yet what you want your contribution to be? This book will help! Stay receptive and bring your open-hearted curiosity.

Training your brain, the power of habits, and introducing power practices

Your brain is incredible!

When a habit is formed, it flows easily, you don't really have to think about it. Now that you've learned how to walk (if you're able) you don't consciously think about it, you just walk.

It can be hard to break old habits, but you can, relatively easily, create new habits. When we're creating a new habit, we're creating new neural pathways in our brains; it can be slow going, as we need to do it consciously. It can feel like bashing a new path through a forest. Over time, and with lots more walkers taking that route, the path gets more established. That's what it's like with habits – over time, and with consistent practice, the new action gets easier, automatic even.

In my work with thousands of leaders over 25 years, I've built a toolkit of tools and techniques which I call 'power practices' – small habits that make a significant tangible difference to your life, little by little, over time – that help you step up without burning out. I've created these practices by integrating ideas from the fields of psychology, performance coaching and spirituality. The power practices I weave throughout this book (and you'll find bonus resources at my site, www.katycatalyst.com/change-makers-book) will help you build healthy mental habits and strong foundations. They're tried and tested and, as you integrate these practices into your life, they can make a big difference to your resilience and wellbeing!

What's coming up? Road map through this book

Chapters 1 and 2 are a whistle-stop tour through key self-awareness concepts as a foundation for the rest of the book. We'll explore our inner dialogue, the purpose of emotions, our bodies' threat responses, thinking errors, developing a growth mindset, befriending our inner critic, listening to our inner wisdom. We'll dig into gratitude, how it helps build our resilience, persistence and impact over time. We'll explore the power of reflection over rumination, our inter-sectional identity as leaders, and how we can embrace more self-compassion through the seasons of our lives.

Chapter 3 is all about developing your resilience to avoid burnout. You'll create your own energy battery and resilience map, meet your best future self and identify rhythms and routines to set you up for success.

Chapter 4 is about tapping into our desires, what we actually want for our lives, what's the change-making contribution we want to make and why it's so important to notice our progress and our small daily 'wins'.

Chapter 5 is all about focus, setting intentions and your full-body 'yes'.

Chapter 6 unpicks the nuanced mix of workplace barri-ers, blockers, how we navigate the systems we find ourselves in, that we choose to join or to exit, and that we perpetuate. We're dialling up our systemic awareness *alongside* our personal self-awareness, how we can build psychological safety and embed equity in our workplaces. We'll talk about microaggressions and privilege, headwinds and tailwinds, overcoming bias, calling out/in, bystanderism and the differ-ence between intention and impact.

Chapter 7 dials up your impact to shine brightly, explor-ing your visibility and super-charging your relationship ecosystem.

Lastly, in Chapter 8 we'll explore how we stay sustainable as change-making leaders, keeping our compassion, hope and our momentum going. The book closes with your insights, takeaways and next steps.

How to use this book

Follow through each stage of the road map, taking time with each of the exercises, or 'dip in' to scratch a particular itch. You'll find power practices and inspirational change-maker interviews woven throughout.

Each chapter includes:

- **Reflection points**: pause and use these journaling prompts to reflect more deeply on the chapter's themes.
- **Exercises**: diagnostics, guided exercises, visualizations and practical challenges to apply your insights from each chapter to your life.
- **Change-maker progress and action tracker**: summary of your learning and a tracker for your progress.
- **Affirmations**: statements of belief about yourself that usually start with 'I' plus a verb. Affirmations are part of how we can re-code and re-create our brain's neural pathways, to help us start to shift our beliefs about ourselves. Sometimes an affirmation can stretch us beyond our current comfort levels – they can feel a bit aspirational, and that's ok! I've sprinkled affirmations for you at the end of each chapter of this book.
- **Bonus resources**: further reading, a full list of affirmations, audio versions of the visualizations and dowloadable templates of all the power practices are available at my site, www.katycatalyst.com/change-maker-book.

Are you ready to dive in?

I hope I'm already validating your quest for purpose in your work and wider life. That asking 'who am I?' and 'why am I here?' are fantastic questions to be asking.

My job in this book is to walk with you, offering suggestions, provocations and guidance to help you go deeper and sprinkling a healthy dollop of compassion throughout.

May what I share here bring fruit and flourishing for your own change-making leadership, and for those you impact. May my thoughts in this book be a provocation for you, an opportunity to refresh or stir up your thinking, and an invitation to go deeper.

Let's go!

UNWIND REWIND

What's most important for you from this introduction?

Which of my coaching principles most resonate for you? Any surprises here?

How do you find learning new habits? What helps you when you want to learn something new?

Think about your current workplace. Who designed it? Who was it designed for? Whose needs does it suit?

Record your thoughts below or in your journal.

....

....

....

....

....

CHAPTER ONE

Change-making wisdom

'Who are you and why are you here?'

An emotion's only purpose in life is to be felt. ANON

Chapters 1 and 2 give you a whistle-stop tour through key self-awareness concepts. It's the 'inner work' foundation to equip you as change-making leaders and change makers in your workplace. In this chapter we'll unpack what's going on in your inner dialogue, and how tuning into your thinking and feeling gives you essential data!

I'm sharing powerful insights about how your mind, emotions and body are interconnected; we'll look at perceptions, the purpose of emotions, our body's threat response and thinking errors. We'll close the chapter with a beautiful gratitude power practice.

The stories we tell ourselves

Let's start with our **perception** and run an experiment together.

EXERCISE   Perception

Jesse is travelling on a bus. Can you picture her? Allow your mind to picture her right now. What does she look like? What is she wearing? Where is she travelling to? What story does your brain give you about this particular woman? Is she like you?

Now let me give you more information about Jesse and let's see what happens to your mental image of her.

As I already mentioned, Jesse is riding on the bus.

Jesse is swinging her legs and admiring her pink wellies, clutching a teddy bear in her arms.

Can you see Jesse? What does she look like now?

Let me tell you something more about Jesse.

Jesse is so excited to see her grand-daughter Ali again.

Jesse hasn't seen Ali for many months, as Jesse's only just returned from her round-the-world sailing trip.

Ok, let's debrief that mini brain experiment.

What happened to your image of Jesse? Did her identity change as you worked through that story?

How old was she at the beginning of the story? What did she look like?

How old is she in your mind now? What does she look like?

I start by seeing a woman like me, then a small kid with pigtails, then an old granny, stooped, with a walking stick and headscarf, then a super-toned gran wearing Lycra!

How about you?

Notice how your image of Jesse shifts. Notice how when you get a piece of data ('she's on the bus', 'she's wearing wellies') your brain fills in the gaps.

This is how bias and perception work. Your brain will choose from data that's already stored and you're most familiar with; it will pattern match. Here's a granny… oh, grannies wear headscarves! You and I may share some stereotypical perceptions of grannies, so we may have had some similar images pop into our minds. And your brain will have given you data and imagery, unique to you and your experience of grannies… and buses… and wellies… and so on.

Notice then how the story your brain gives you (which includes all kinds of assumptions and biases) affects your perception of reality.

I share this exercise with you to demonstrate how malleable our perception of reality is, how we can shape and tell *multiple versions* of a story.

Our own version of a story will likely be *very believable* to us. The story we're telling ourselves also shapes the experiences we have. We can change the story we're telling ourselves, and see what difference that makes to what we're experiencing.

When I ask 'where are you?' notice how you can answer that question in so many different ways. You can answer it in terms of geography and location ('I'm currently in Scotland'), you can be more specific ('I'm at Rannoch Road in Edinburgh') and you can get even more precise ('I'm in the kitchen cooking pasta').

You can answer the question 'where are you?' in a way that reflects your emotions. 'I'm a little lost right now' or 'I'm feeling really settled'.

You can answer 'where are you?' in terms of where you feel you're at more broadly in life, for example 'I'm at the stage of life where I'm questioning everything', 'I'm wanting to settle down' or 'I'm restless for more adventure…'.

REFLECTION POINT

What's the story you're telling yourself about where you're at?

How does the story you're telling yourself affect how you feel?

How does the story you're telling yourself affect the meaning that you're giving to your situation?

....
....
....
....
....

Through this book I'm inviting you to be open to some new stories, some new interpretations.

At the same time, our perceptions are also shaped by strong societal conditioning, which forms biases, pre-judgements and prejudices in our minds, and creates cultural norms across society. We often don't see how much these factors have conditioned us and are shaping us so strongly.

Through this book I'm inviting you to be open to seeing and noticing this conditioning, so that you can start to unlearn it, and step up in your change-making leadership.

Let's dive into some deeper self-discovery and self-awareness.

Tuning into your thoughts and feelings

Tuning into your inner dialogue is foundational for your wellbeing and change-making skillset. This may be new or a refresher for you – notice what your inner dialogue wants to say to you about that!

This gratitude power practice demonstrates how powerful our thoughts are to affect how we feel, and then how we show up. Read it through first before you close your eyes! Or ask a friend to lead you through it.

POWER PRACTICE   Gratitude

Find an undisturbed space, close your eyes.

Take a few slow breaths. Notice where your breath enters and leaves your body.

Every time there's a new thought or a distraction, just bring your attention back to your breath.

Do this for a few moments.

Feel your body relax.

Bring to your mind three things that you're grateful for. They can be big, medium, small, doesn't matter.

Hold those three things in your mind.

Notice what you start to *feel*, as you think about those three things.

Let your body flood with those feelings. Enjoy a few moments lingering here. Relish the feelings.

Hold your three things in your mind for a moment longer.

Breathe deeply.

When you're ready, wiggle your fingers and toes, open your eyes gently, and come back into your room.

How was that exercise?

What did you feel when you thought about the three things you're grateful for?

How do you feel now?

Notice you can shift how you're *feeling*, based on what you're *thinking* and what you focus your attention on. This is powerful, right?

When I run this gratitude exercise I usually feel calm and present, then I feel happiness and joy wash through me, and I leave feeling energized and refreshed. I also notice that after this exercise my thinking is crisper and my mind feels clearer, it's like a windscreen wiper across my brain. It's amazing!

Let's imagine you're working on a high-profile project with a colleague you find annoying. We'll call him Bert. You're preparing for your client update meeting, mulling over and thinking about the long list of things that irritate you about Bert. Pause a moment. Notice how you're feeling? Annoyed, frustrated, tense, apprehensive… right? Now think about how this thinking and feeling will *affect how you show up* in your client meeting.

These feelings will leak out in your behaviours. You're likely to be less open and receptive to Bert, maybe even with your client. This may impact how you two come across in your meeting and how you're able to influence the client. This may ultimately impact the success of your project and your work reputation.

Let's imagine that Bert arrives at your meeting late and blanks you. What are the various thoughts you can have in response, and how do they affect how you feel and act (Table 1.1)?

TABLE 1.1 Linking our thinking, feelings and behaviours

What you think	What you feel	How you act next
He's so rude! I'm being treated unreasonably and I won't stand for it.	Angry	Blank him back, ignore him in the meeting.
What have I done to offend him? I'm in danger and I won't be able to cope with it.	Anxiety	Worry inside your own head. Make yourself smaller, hold back.
Maybe he knows something about the client and he's keeping it from me.	Suspicious	Act defensively.
I thought we were friends!	Sadness	Think about all the good times you've lost.

(continued)

TABLE 1.1 (Continued)

What you think	What you feel	How you act next
Oh no, he must have heard me criticize him to my colleague!	Guilt	Avoid eye contact, keep out of his way.
He doesn't value me, I'm not good enough.	Shame	Think about all the other times you've failed or how much of a failure you are.

You can play out how your ensuing behaviours might impact your performance in the meeting and the impression you make on your client!

And yet, what if I told you that Bert received some troubling family news, just before stepping into the meeting? His reaction wasn't anything to do with you; he was just doing his best to be present and hold it together. His behaviour wasn't about you!

This exercise shows us how malleable our thoughts are. How our brains can easily provide a story that can seem very accurate and believable to us, and yet can be entirely inaccurate! We can spiral into rumination. Our thoughts can stimulate feelings that provoke more interpretations, and in a series of split seconds we're in a downward spiral of doom and gloom, or 'shoulds' and 'oughts'. Do you recognize how often you create unnecessary dramas in your mind?!

Your thoughts are automatic and they lie! They're very believable, because they're yours. Learning to question your automatic response to thoughts is a practice to improve brain function, mental health and wellbeing. These split-second shifts of thinking and feeling can feel very uncontrollable, but we can learn to tune in and just notice without judgement.[1]

Let's add another layer and **let's get emotional!** Check in with your feelings using the following reflection point.

REFLECTION POINT

Notice what emotions you've felt so far today. Take your pick from this selection (there are many more!):[2]

Boredom, contentment, depression, hopefulness, frustration, grief/loss, optimism, fear, delight, impatience, anticipation, appreciation, enthusiasm, doubt, blame, shame, jealousy, anger, pride, sadness, discouragement.

Notice the range of emotion, hour by hour, moment by moment.

Notice the ebb and flow of your emotions.

Notice the intensity.

Which feelings are missing from this list?

Which of these feelings have you judged as 'bad'?

Which of these feelings have you judged as 'good'?

Which of these feelings are most comfortable or uncomfortable for you?

....

....

....

....

....

All our emotions have data for us. We can ignore, deny, repress, but because our minds, bodies, spirits and emotions are interconnected, they'll likely come up some other way, leaking out in our behaviours, as we saw above with Bert, in our blind spots and 'shadow side', or repressed in our bodies and even manifesting as illness.[3]

Emotions as dashboard data

What happens when we start to see emotion purely as *data*, as *indicators* for ourselves, like a dashboard? Neither good nor bad, neither right nor wrong. Just giving us information, helping us notice things. For example, when you feel anger, what is it trying to tell you? How about guilt? Shame? Emotions may carry messages and functions for us.[4]

Use Table 1.2 to explore what they might be.

See how useful this is, when we notice something in our bodies, to interrogate it a little further. It reveals a feeling, we ask the feeling: what are you wanting to tell me, what is my need here?

How do we know what we're feeling if we've learned to shun, deny, hide, numb out (or many other strategies of avoidance) our feelings? The power practices throughout this book will support you to notice how you embody particular feelings and connect with the feelings in your body. Chapter 3 will support you in identifying your energy fluctuations In Chapters 4 and 5 we'll explore what data your desires, joy and full-body 'yes' and even your jealousy have for you. Juicy stuff!

TABLE 1.2 What do our emotions tell us?

Message	Emotion/feeling	Purpose/function
Anticipate future threat	Anxiety	Protects me
My expectations of how other people should behave are violated	Anger	Something important to me is blocked
I'm experiencing reward and this activity is giving me meaning	Happiness	I'm being consistent with my values – reminding me to do this again!
Anticipating reward	Excitement	Seek pleasure and do things that give me a reward
I've violated the rules I hold for myself	Guilt	Keeps me aligned/ self-regulating
I've been revealed to myself or others that I'm not up to the mark/I'm defective in some way	Shame	Purpose of shame is contested[5]
My values of how I think others should treat me have been violated	Hurt	Asserting my needs in a relationship
I want something that somebody else has got	Jealousy	Motivational force to meet my own needs and desires

(continued)

TABLE 1.2 (Continued)

Message	Emotion/feeling	Purpose/function
I've lost something, tells me the value of the thing I lost	Sadness	I might care for this thing differently in the future or how I'll replace that need in the future

1 **Our bodies hold the data!** Our feelings are embodied.[6] We can tune in to listen.
2 **Feelings themselves are neutral.** They're not right or wrong. Some feelings can be very uncomfortable for us, particularly if we've not learned to accept them, to feel them.
3 **Let's not judge our feelings.** They're responses to thoughts in our brain, which are chemical reactions in response to a stimulus. Our feelings have valuable data for us if we tune in and listen.
4 **Our judgements are linked to conditioning.** We've often soaked up social conditioning around what feelings are ok and what feelings are good or bad. For example, girls tend to pick up messaging that it's not ok to be angry. Boys tend to pick up messaging that it's not ok to be sad.[7] In many workplaces we've picked up messages that expressing any emotions is misplaced or irrelevant!
5 **Feelings pass** – in just 90 seconds![8] Tune into it. Feel it. Let it pass. Often, it's the meaning and interpretation we put on our feelings that mean they linger and we start to

ruminate (see Chapter 2). It's the interpretations, and the sense we make, that impact our resilience.[9]

6 **It's how we act on our emotions that creates the positive or negative consequences.** We hold responsibility for our actions and our behaviours.

Your inner dialogue, enabling beliefs + limiting beliefs

Your brain is constantly in dialogue – you're having conversations with yourself! As well as listening to our bodies' data, we can start to tune into our inner dialogue as a useful source of data. As you listen in, you'll start to hear some of your core beliefs – thoughts you hold to be true about yourself (your abilities, your capacity) and about others:

· *Enabling beliefs* expand you and help you step up. They're realistic, positive judgements, about who you are and what you're capable of.
· *Limiting beliefs* focus on what you think you can't do or can't be. Limiting beliefs hold you back from fulfilling your potential and stepping up as you may wish to do.

Tuning in to hear these beliefs that're running, and seeing how these serve you, or whether there are any beliefs you'd like to change, is dynamite in your change-making leadership. You're getting to know yourself and seeing how you can use your mind to support you as you step up. Remember you are powerful and this is a key source and access point to your power!

Your brain's threat response and negativity bias

Your brain scans for threats, and it's hypervigilant in order to keep you safe. We register social threat in the same way we register physical threat,[10] which kicks off our 'threat response', triggering our body's sympathetic nervous system and readying us for survival. We prepare for fight, flight (run away), freeze (shut down), appease (fawn or be compliant) or flock (find others for protection!). When our body's in a threat response, which is activated by the limbic part of our brain, then the capacity of the rational part of our brain, called the pre-frontal cortex, is reduced. This means we're more vulnerable to thinking errors, otherwise known as bias.

Our threat response leads to our brains having a *negativity bias*. We lock onto, remember and literally develop stronger neural pathways around negative thoughts and experiences. When we're processing our day before bed, we tend to remember the negative experiences, the uncomfortable feelings or high-pressure moments. Power practices are designed to do some re-wiring for you! Focusing on positive joy-filled moments – not because I'm advocating 'fake positivity' or 'fake-it-till-you-make-it' – enables there to be a balance.[11]

Thinking errors

When we're in threat response we're more susceptible to thinking errors.[12] These are thought patterns that can become habits.

We may *over-generalize*, fall into *all-or-nothing* thinking (if I'm not perfect I've failed, either I do it right or not at all), *jump to conclusions*, *disqualify* and discount the positive things that happened or that you or others have done (that doesn't count because…). We may get into *mind reading* (imagining we know what others are thinking), *emotional reasoning* where we assume that because we feel a certain way, what we think must be true (I feel embarrassed so I must actually be a failure). We can *personalize*, blaming ourselves or taking responsibility for something that's not our fault, or blaming others when we were responsible. *Hindsight* or *past event* bias causes us to look back and see events that have already occurred as more predictable than is actually the case. When we assign *labels* to ourselves or other people (I'm a failure, I'm useless, they're an idiot) and *language* like 'should', 'ought', 'must', 'always', 'never', these are indicators that we're in thinking error. These words can make us feel guilty, or like we've already failed, and if we apply 'shoulds' to other people the result is often frustration.

These are micro-moments of brain activity but can lead to further interpretations and feelings that shape our behaviours.

These biases are all forms of *selective attention*: the unconscious part of our minds paying attention to part of, or certain types of, evidence and failing to pay attention to the rest. For example, we might notice our own or others' failures but not see progress and success. We miss information that could disprove our belief, so we continue to believe something incorrect or unhelpful. Selective attention acts like a mental filter; we miss out on the full picture. We only take in biased selection of evidence, can only make a biased interpretation, and then store a biased memory of what happened.

What are the implications of these thinking errors? Can you see how thinking errors, aka bias, can affect the **stories you're telling yourself**, and therefore how you **feel** about yourself, your own change-making or leadership capacity, and then how that can affect how you show up and **behave** at work? This is a key piece of awareness when you want to step up without burning out!

Going back to your meeting with Bert from earlier: what thinking errors are running when you're thinking about all the things that irritate you about him? I can spot *selective attention* (you're not seeing the evidence of the work he does well), *all-or-nothing* ('it's either him or me!'), *personalization* ('there must be something wrong with me if we're not getting on'). I'm hearing some 'shoulds' and 'oughts' as well! When these errors are running, you're in threat response and your wise, rational, compassionate mind is impaired. More than this, you'll be scanning selectively for any additional evidence to 'prove' your opinion of Bert. This is how bias clouds our judgement and affects our decision making (without us realizing). Notice, too, how your negativity bias can lead you down a path of rumination ('let me scan through all the memories of when I've not got on with other colleagues or when other relationships haven't gone well' and so on), which affects your mood and how you show up.

EXERCISE   Bias check-in

Which thinking errors do you recognize? (NB: We tend to struggle to immediately notice these for ourselves, so this requires some tuning in!)

What are the implications when these thinking biases are at play?

- For you and your beliefs about yourself?
- For your confidence, self-belief and willingness to step up in your change making?
- For your leadership?
- Within your team?
- Within your workplace?

When we become aware of our thinking errors and the biases they create, what can we do to find alternative thinking?

Choose one of the thinking errors you recognize. What might be an alternative way to think, to help you manage this bias within yourself?

We'll come back to thinking errors when we talk about our inner critic in Chapter 2 and when we look at workplace and organizational bias in Chapter 6.

So, now that we know more about how our brains work, and how our thinking affects how we feel, which affects how we show up, what can we do about it?

Resetting your central nervous system

The power practices throughout this book are designed to strengthen your resilience by resetting your central nervous system – to access your body's *parasympathetic nervous system* and enable your body's self-soothe or 'relaxation response' to kick in. This counteracts your body's 'threat response' and means that your brain is less vulnerable to thinking errors.

This breathing power practice is a super simple startpoint – give it a go!

POWER PRACTICE Breathing

Find somewhere comfortable to sit, start to put your attention on your body, notice how you're sitting… stretch out any tension.

> Then put your attention on to the breath.
>
> Notice where the breath enters and leaves your body.
>
> Extend your inhale, breathe in deeply.
>
> Extend your exhale, you can even 'sigh' it out. Do that a few more times.

You can imagine your breath going to the very bottom of your lungs, to the middle of your backbone. I open up my arms to make a bit more space for my lungs to expand!

Notice that your mind will likely be chattering with other thoughts; just bring your attention back to the breath each

---

time you notice that your thoughts are elsewhere. Be gentle with yourself here. It's really normal for our minds to be very chatty. This is a practice!

Take a few more lovely, deep breaths.

Notice how your body starts to feel as your breath slows and steadies.

Do you notice a calm feeling, a heavy feeling? Just notice.

Activating your body's relaxation response, as Tamu Thomas, somatic coach and founder of Live Three Sixty, calls your 'system safety', is essential to regulating your nervous system and has a massive array of wider health benefits: slowing heart rate, reducing blood pressure, relieving stress and anxiety.[13] Now you know how to do this, you can use this anytime you want to shift into a calm, relaxed or more focused state.[14]

Tamu shares that:

what I need, and we all need, is to centre ourselves and our wholeness. When we do that – when we're not stuck in survival mode physiology, it ripples out for others. I'm no longer in scarcity – the more I share, the more there is. We think it's frivolous, we think this is for expensive 'active wear women' who go to retreats all day long. Because we're brought up in a culture of toxic shame, where the things that make us human are perceived as inconvenient and shameful, we shame ourselves and assume others will shame us as well, when we say this is what we need.

How else can we activate our relaxation response?

So many ancient wisdom traditions, religious faith and sacred practices have this central nervous system reset at the heart of regular practices. Prayer, worship, meditation, chanting – all can help us access a trance-like state. We can also access this flow-like state when we're sharing a moment of collective consciousness in experiences such as a music festival, worship service or football match.[15]

Once we shift out of threat response, our brains are able to access our rational thinking and we can choose to give a more healthy and accurate thinking response. Tamu shared this example of how seeking system safety can benefit us in the workplace:

> It's not 'I'm not good enough because I can't do back-to-back meetings or stay until midnight like everybody else'. If you're in a workplace that tolerates and promotes back-to-back meetings (which doesn't work for who we are and how we are), take a moment to check in with your breath, take a moment to allow your nervous system to calm itself. Then you can start to say 'can I have 10 minutes space between meetings' or set up your own appointments for lunch breaks.
>
> When we experience system safety – in our bodies, not our minds – then we develop our competency to meet our own needs. That competency enables you to say to your manager: 'I've been experimenting…. I've found I'm much more effective and much more alert when I've 10 mins in between meetings – can we make that happen?'
>
> Who's going to say no to that?!

All the power practices in this book are designed to reset your nervous system, access your body's relaxation response and shift your emotional state. We'll do more on this when we tune in to hear our inner wisdom in Chapter 2, when we build out our resilience in Chapter 3, and find flow in Chapter 5.

Coming back to your meeting with Bert: what would happen if you switched from a focus on him and his perceived flaws, to a focus instead on your own resilience? If you took a moment to focus on your breath, give attention to the affirmations 'I am powerful, I can choose my response, I'm able to handle this situation, this guy annoys me but I can stay calm, I can achieve our goal'? What shifts in your physiology and in your emotions as you shift your attention in this way? How do you feel: calmer, more powerful... right?

Unwind rewind: chapter summary

Your brain is powerful! You can train your brain to create new healthy mental habits for yourself, and these are critical in your quest to step up without burning out.

In this chapter we've explored how perceptions and bias affect our experience of reality, and gone deeper into noticing our inner dialogue, so that we can tune in, notice how our thoughts affect how we feel, and how we then choose to behave. We've explored how feelings carry essential data for us, how our brain's negativity bias and threat response can exacerbate thinking errors, and how to activate our body's relaxation response.

These new habits build our resilience, using the power of our mind to shape our experience of reality, and are key pieces to resource our change-making leadership. We'll be building on these insights through Chapter 2 as we talk about deepening your growth mindset and listening to your inner wisdom. We'll also explore your sense of identity in your leadership and have a reality check on where you are in this season of your life. In Chapter 4 we'll build on these insights as we tune into our desires and focus on our change-making contribution.

Let's close this chapter with a power practice that counteracts our negativity bias and resets our central nervous system, for a soothing end-of-day. Pick an affirmation from the list below.

POWER PRACTICE   End of day close

Breathe slowly.

Bring to mind three things today that you are proud of.

That you contributed to.

That you found beautiful, fun, inspiring or funny.

Add your affirmation. Know that you are loved.

Breathe.

UNWIND REWIND

What's most important for you from this chapter?

Which thinking errors do you recognize?

Which power practices will you experiment with, to build your healthy mental habits?

Which affirmation are you choosing?

Record your thoughts in your change-maker progress + action tracker or your journal.

YOUR CHANGE-MAKER PROGRESS + ACTION TRACKER

- This is what I'm experimenting with (action I'm taking to make a difference).
- This is what I'm noticing.
- Here's what I'm going to do with what I'm learning.
- Here's how I'll keep myself going.
- Here's how I'll stay accountable.

AFFIRMATIONS

'I am enough.'

'I have enough.'

'I do enough.'

'My work is good enough.'

'I am capable. I am powerful. I have talents and gifts to share.'

'I am wise. I can trust and I have all I need to make good choices.'

'I can be the whole, authentic, amazing version of myself.'

CHANGE MAKER INTERVIEW Davinia Tomlinson

Davinia Tomlinson *is the award-winning founder of rainchq, a business designed to help women build sustainable long-term wealth and live life on their own terms – unapologetically. She's building a thriving community of rainmakers across the globe, filled with women who inspire, uplift and support other women in real life.*

I talked with Davinia about her change making in the finance industry, how she's disrupting the system and keeps on smiling!

I'm a change maker because I believe in my ability to identify a problem that affects me and the people around me, devise a practical solution and most importantly to do something about it, while inspiring others to join me along the way. I'm passionate, in the truly madly deeply sense, about seeing women win, specifically through building wealth to live life entirely on their own terms. I believe that for women, financial self-care is the most radical act of self-love.

I'm motivated by the ongoing economic inequalities that plague women and mean that we have to work even harder than we already do to improve our life outcomes. With a gender pensions gap which could potentially mean the average UK woman retiring with a pension pot just one-fifth of the size of those of our male counterparts, and a gender pay gap which persists decades after the introduction of the Equal Pay Act in the UK, a gap made worse if you're a woman of colour and exacerbated by motherhood, it's clear that individual action alone is inadequate to tackle these issues. Governmental and institutional-level action is essential too. It's no surprise that in 2021, UN Women said that the events of the previous 12 months could set gender equality back 25 years. A horrifying thought.

On resilience

Resilience for me relates to the infrastructure I put in place to cope with life's shocks, whether that be financial, emotional, physical or anything else. It doesn't involve striving for a life of perfection, but putting the systems in place to safeguard my wellbeing and mitigate, as much as possible, the impact of life's unplanned-for events.

It doesn't mean never tripping up – it just means getting up as quickly and as painlessly as possible, assessing where the pothole was and learning how to avoid it in future

On 'creating new tables'

The entire basis of my business is centred around building my own table in the finance world at which all women, irrespective of age, race or background gain access to high-quality, empathetic financial education and advice specifically to help them achieve their vision for their lives, whatever that looks like for them.

With study after study demonstrating the huge financial inequalities women face, many of which continue to widen, you don't need to be an expert to see that the status quo is a fail.

It's a real privilege to be making a contribution to permanently reversing this trend. The ripple effect of women exercising full financial agency on local communities, society and the economy in general cannot be overstated.

On dealing with opposition to your change-making work

When I was first setting up my business, I did a huge amount of research among the target audience to test what appetite there might be for a female-focused finance solution delivered by women, for women. While the overwhelming majority were supporters, there were some women who were at best lukewarm and at worst insulted by the prospect of what they considered to be a segregated approach to their financial affairs.

Then there were the men who told me the market for female-focused finance was too small and that the only way to be a success was to open up the business to everyone rather than to be focused. It taught me my first business lesson: having the courage of my convictions and holding my nerve. A lesson that's been crucial given the line of work I'm in, helping women to transform their financial futures, partly, through levelling up their self-confidence and flipping their money mindset. After all, the only way to help anyone become a rainmaker is to be a rainmaker myself!

On being ourselves

Being my fully authentic self is not only my biggest USP but also my superpower. I was fortunate enough to receive this advice throughout my upbringing by my staunchly fierce and feminist late dad, who commanded me to always speak up and never to shrink, and this was then reinforced early in my twenties by a senior leader in my first graduate job.

It went on to shape how I perceived my contribution and value both in the workplace and as a business owner, particularly given the multitude of potential pitfalls for a young woman of colour in a notoriously white, notoriously male industry. It's one of the greatest gifts I hope to give to some of the younger women I'm fortunate enough to work with and is, I believe, a lesson that will last them a lifetime.

CHAPTER TWO

Change-making self-awareness

'Where are you?'

If you do not intentionally, deliberately and
proactively include, you will unintentionally
exclude. ANNIE JEAN-BAPTISTE[1]

We're continuing our whistle-stop tour through key self-discovery concepts as foundations for your change-making leadership. In this chapter we'll unpack growth mindset and how to develop it, the concept of our inner critic and how to befriend it, and how we tap into our inner wisdom and create space to listen to ourselves more deeply. We'll highlight the power of reflection over rumination. We'll also see how our inner dialogue is shaped and reinforced by our cultural and societal conditioning (with more to come in Chapter 6). I'm convinced most of us can be more self-compassionate in our inner dialogue, so I'm sprinkling a healthy dollop of that throughout!

We'll explore our intersectional identity as leaders, and how we can honour the seasons of our lives.

Tuning in

Nurturing your growth mindset

Dr Carol Dweck conducted a meta study of what creates happiness and success for humans. She boiled down a complex set of data points to a very simple yet profound model, contrasting 'fixed' and 'growth' mindset:[2]

> When we're in *fixed mindset* we hold a binary way of perceiving our talent, capability and potential. I am either creative or good at spreadsheets, or I'm not. I'm either sporty or musical, or I'm not. I avoid challenge as it may expose my weaknesses or deficiencies. Failure is devastating because it exposes my lack of something. Others' success is threatening. Fixed mindset is rooted in *lack*.
>
> *Growth mindset* says that our talent, capacity and potential are exponentially extendable. That I can learn, grow and change. That I can develop my creativity, Excel skills, sportiness or musical appreciation. Mistakes and failure are opportunities for learning. Others' success is an opportunity for inspiration, to see what may be possible for me. Challenge and obstacles are ways in which I learn and grow. Growth mindset is rooted in *abundance*.

Dr Dweck uses the phrase 'not yet'. 'I'm not yet super skilled at… I'm getting there, I'm learning, I'm giving myself grace.'[3] Our growth mindset is a wonderful asset to draw on, particularly as we go deeper in this book in understanding our own implications in systems, how we perpetuate systems, how bias exists in us, how we navigate and dismantle. We will be 'called out' and 'called in' in our change-making work, and our growth mindset is going to help!

I talked with Audacity Coach Keri Jarvis about her change-making purpose and I was struck by her growth mindset:

> I'm a change maker because I can't believe I was fooled for so long that everything is basically fine! Eight years into a feminist awakening, I'm still learning about injustices I'd never considered. We can't wait to be experts, we must share and act on what we know now. I want to look back on my career and cringe at things I used to say and do, because then I'll know I've really maxed out on learning and growth.

Stop 'shoulding' on yourself – your inner critic and how to recognize it

Our *inner critic* is a psychological process whereby our brain keeps us safe – it's a functional part of being human! By pointing out the things that could go wrong, it exposes the risks inherent in a particular situation or decision, or ways that we've messed up.[4] Our inner critic also serves to keep us small. If we allow our inner critic to be too loud, distracting or dominant, it can really hold us back.[5]

The inner critic can take on different tones or emphases. Here are some examples:

- The inner critic can show up as a **perfectionist,** telling us that we ourselves, and our work, aren't good enough. This voice discourages us from putting ourselves and our work out there, for fear of rejection, disapproval or not meeting the ever-present high standards. We procrastinate and put off important pieces of work, or are so distracted by detail that we miss the bigger-picture opportunities.

- The inner critic can show up with lots of **rules and boundaries** to keep us safe, holding us back and keeping us small, so that we don't embarrass or make a fool of ourselves. When we listen to this voice, we constrain ourselves and limit what we even believe we're capable of.

- The inner critic can show up with a strong **work-hard** driving quality, perpetuating the belief that we'll only keep ourselves safe if we push ourselves and maintain high standards. This can sap our joy, our delight, and mean we don't connect with what's most important to us, nor value rest and pleasure in our lives.

- The inner critic can show up with a strong **conforming** emphasis. This critic wants us to fit in with others' expectations, so that we're not rejected or excluded by them and left out of the 'in-group'. These are the rules, this is how you fit in, this is how you conform to society's (or family, workplace, social group or beauty) standards and expectations, and you mustn't stray for fear of being rejected by the group.

POWER PRACTICE   Recognizing your inner critic

Tune into your inner dialogue. How are you speaking to yourself?

Look out for words like 'should', 'ought', 'always', 'never'.

How does your inner critic show up?

Which of these characteristics do you recognize from your own inner dialogue?

....
....
....
....
....

This can be a massive 'aha!' moment for clients – this voice has been so present, and so believable, for so long, that we didn't even know it wasn't a permanent fixture! I notice that the activists, change makers and conscious leaders that I coach can have very loud inner critics, often with strong work-hard and perfectionist flavours. The commitment and core value to make a difference can override our attention to our own wellbeing, creativity and joy. It can be a huge revelation and relief to discover that you can shift these patterns and reduce the inner critic's domination! This can be absolutely life changing for many women leaders I know.

The inner critic perpetuates our thinking errors, strengthening the neural pathways and ways that our brains can fall into bias, which we discussed in Chapter 1. Our brain is wired for the inner critic to be heard loudly and these thoughts develop into thinking habits, which are reinforced and conditioned in and through society's messaging. For example, girls are taught to conform through schools' reward and punishment systems, and young women learn to hold back for fear of being the 'tall poppy' or being 'too big for her boots'.[6] I argue that we can work consciously and intentionally to dial the inner critic down. I'm going to show you how to do that (once I've introduced you to your inner wisdom).

Before we move on from our inner critic, I invite you to consider what your inner critic reveals for you. When we tune into it, we can start to hear the underlying beliefs that govern us, the rules by which we live our lives. This is super-helpful and revealing in allowing us to understand our motivations and our inner workings as change makers and as leaders. Noticing how our inner critic is showing up, and understanding the root of that, is also the start-point for reducing its power over us!

Your inner wisdom and how to tap into it

Your inner dialogue also includes the voice of your inner guide, reflecting your deeper wisdom. This part of you is infinitely kind, compassionate and wise, knows you intimately and sees your potential. This voice encourages and supports you, and is your inner cheerleader! When you connect with your inner wisdom, you're likely to feel clear, aligned, at peace, connected. You're tuning into your intuition. This voice may be a very small quiet voice, even a whisper at times. Sometimes your inner wisdom speaks in words, sometimes in senses, images, perceptions, even

jumping to conclusions ('client won't ask us back!'), my *selective attention* is filtering out all the positive feedback we'd received ('doesn't count!') and I'm *personalizing* the situation ('this was bad, so I must be bad at this'). The rumination is feeding my inner critic; the thoughts are triggering more and more negative emotions and spinning out further limiting beliefs about myself. Not fun!

Has this ever happened to you?!

Rumination is the mental process whereby we go over and over something. This can be focused in the **past** and *regret* based: 'I wish I'd...' 'I should have... 'I ought to have...' Or focused in the **future** and *anxiety or worry* based: 'what if...'. Both can keep us stuck.

Reflection helps us break out of rumination, get really **present**, rather than past or future focused, and shift our state to a more positive one. We access our growth mindset and it's a much healthier, growth-filled place to be. It's a powerful tool to develop.[7]

Interrupting rumination

So, what can we do when the thoughts are churning in the middle of the night? How do we get un-stuck from rumination?

POWER PRACTICE   Shifting out of rumination

1 **Notice** – notice you are ruminating and *stop*! Call time on yourself. I've a friend who allows herself 10 minutes of 'wallowing time' before she calls time out and consciously either moves into a reflection space or moves on.

---

2 **Interrupt** – interrupt the thought process and pattern, get up, move around, shift your physical position, change your focal length to stretch your eye muscles.

3 **Process the feelings** – go for a walk, talk it out with a friend, leave yourself a voice note, write in your journal, name the feelings.

4 **Learning** – use these three golden questions to help you shift out of rumination and into healthy reflection:
   a. What did I learn?
   b. What will I do differently going forward?
   c. What am I grateful for?

5 **Interrogate** – notice the beliefs about yourself that are running underneath this rumination process. Where are the limiting beliefs? Where are the enabling beliefs?

6 **Affirmations** – use them to help you shift your beliefs.

Stepping up in our leadership and change-maker identity

Your intersectional identity

Let's consider who you are as a change maker and change-making leader.

What aspects of your identity show up in your leadership? How are you bringing yourself into your leadership? The intersectionality map, illustrated by Sakina Saidi and shown in Figure 2.1, is based on the work of Kimberle Crenshaw[8] and Patricia Hill Collins[9] and allows us to see and hold the various aspects of who we are and the layers

FIGURE 2.1 Intersectionality map

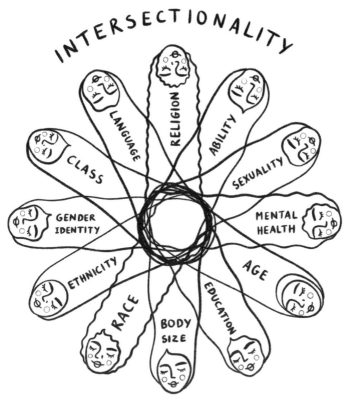

of our identity. As well as affecting how we show up in our workplaces and wider world, our intersectional identity also affects our lived experiences in the workplace and moving around the world.[10]

A note about privilege. If we hold aspects of identity that 'fit' inside the 'norm', akin to the 'default' leader that's dominant in our workplace cultures, for example male, white, cis-gendered, heteronormative, neurotypical, able-bodied, we'll experience privilege, or unearned advantage. If we hold aspect(s) of our identity that fall outside of these norms, we'll likely experience being excluded, bending out of shape to fit in, or being in an 'out-group'.[11] Where we deviate from the 'norm' there may be extra work to do to accept and appreciate who we are and the stage of life we're in. These dynamics can be subtle, changing according to context and situation. Or they can be very blatant, obvious and clear. We'll explore more in Chapter 6.

Your intersectionality map

Use Figure 2.1 to explore your own intersectionality map.

REFLECTION POINT

How would you describe yourself using aspects of this intersectionality map?

What's easy to talk about?

What's harder to talk about?

Which aspects of your identity are visible to the outside world? Which are invisible?

Which aspects do you leave out? Or don't bring into work? Where do you 'censor' yourself? Can you dig a little deeper and explore why that is?

....

....

....

....

....

This chapter is all about deepening our self-awareness, to support us in our change-making leadership. Let's use the metaphor now of seasons of our life to go deeper into our 'where are you?' question.

Seasons of your life

There are seasons of our lives and in our growth. There are seasons in nature, in the climate and months as they pass by. We can parallel seasons in our work projects, in our energy and in our menstrual cycles:[12]

Spring is the season of new beginnings, with a fresh energy.
Summer is the season of visibility, flourishing and fruitfulness.
Autumn is the season of culmination, bringing a detail orientation.
Winter is the season of rest, recuperation, healing, evaluation.

Each of the seasons has a distinctive energy that it brings, before starting the cycle again! There are multiple ways we can use this lens of seasons to bring insight to our question 'Where are you?'

You can think about the **seasons in terms of your life overall**. For example, the early decades of life emerge into Spring, in the middle years you're in Summer bloom through to Autumn, and the later stages of life are late Autumn into Winter.

You can think about the **climatic seasons as they shift and change each year** and what each season brings (of course, with different nuance, colour and variety, depending on where you live and whether you are in the northern or southern hemisphere). I live in northwest England where I love the fact that the seasons are generally quite pronounced. The long light days, vibrancy and warmth of Summer are often quite short (!), I love the beautiful rich colours of Autumn as the trees change, that Winter is cold and dark, often with snow and frost, and that Spring brings bursts of colour from Spring flowers and new-born lambs. We can create our lives around the seasons and what each season requires of us; each season has its own essence and beauty.

You can think about **seasons of a project or piece of work**. Every project (if it's to be successful!) goes through essential stages. There's a stage of inception with early creation and planning, there's a stage of design and mapping out the route to come (Spring), there's a stage of delivery and making it all happen (Summer), there's a stage of wrapping up and making sure you've got the results (Autumn) and there's a pause to evaluate and re-centre (Winter), before you start all over again. Often, of course, we're running multiple projects at once, and therefore experiencing the energy of multiple seasons at any one time.

Living in sync with the seasons

What happens, what starts to shift, when we begin to live with increased intention and attention paid to the seasons?

Living seasonally and cyclically is counter-cultural to our (predominantly Western) society's A–B linear focus and 'hustle' culture. This culture tells us that we need to always be 'on', always 'push' and always 'go'. Personal and societal wellbeing is not valued or, at best, your self-care is designed to enable you to pep up your energy, just enough so you can keep going with the hustle and grind. Your value in the workplace is in your productivity and your output.

When you start to connect with your embodied energy day by day, week by week, month by month, you'll likely notice that your energy is not linear and always 'on'; there are ebbs and flows.

Living more seasonally and cyclically pays attention to these ebbs and flows, acknowledging that we need 'down' and 'off' time as well as 'up' and 'on' time. When we look at nature and the natural world, we see this beautifully modelled for us. Nature doesn't force or constantly push, and yet everything grows and blooms at its own pace.

Change-making work is often hard, messy, complex and takes a lot of energy! We'll burn out if we have expectations that we'll always be 'out' and 'on'. We need to learn to pace ourselves and bring balance. Living and working cyclically and more in tune with the seasons is transformational in building our resilience, and helps us make our contribution in a sustainable way.

For now, just notice what season of life you are in, using the following reflection point.

REFLECTION POINT

1 What season of your overall life are you in: Spring, Summer, Autumn, Winter?

2 What season are you in for specific areas of your life:
   a. Your business/your career overall?
   b. Your family life?

c. Particular work projects?

d. Relationships that are important to you?

3 What energy do you notice? What's energizing? What's draining?

4 Where do you spend most of your time energetically – do you feel like you're 'always on' (Spring into Summer, for example)?

5 What seasons in the cycle do you give less attention to, or even miss out completely?

....
....
....
....
....

Working with the seasons, there are a few things to notice:

1 We can be in one season in one aspect of our life, and another season in another.

2 The cycles can go at different speeds, for different aspects of our lives.

3 This isn't about fully embracing the energy of one particular season at the expense of other responsibilities requiring a different kind of energy. That's unrealistic!

4 How can we honour the seasons we're in? Even 10% of intentional activity aligned to that season can make a big difference.

5 Try attending to each season each week, or take yourself on a cycle each day.

STORY Living cyclically in work and business

My business can be in Summer and needing me in full 'on' mode, connecting with others, getting visible on social media or podcasts and running client workshops, where I hold space for lots of people. It takes a lot of *out*ward energy. Meanwhile I may be in my menstrual phase with my body and inner energy in Winter. In this situation I need to balance the needs of my body's '*in*wards' energy with the needs of my business for '*out*wards' energy!

At the end of a creative project I can want to jump straight on to the next project, if I'm feeling energized (Spring), or jump straight to the sofa, if I'm feeling drained (Winter). Either way, I miss out on the valuable season of Autumn, with its energy of culmination, to land the project and finish it off well. If I don't give my projects some Autumn focus, I'm storing up problems in my business over time (accounts not up to date, invoices not sent, learning and insights not fully embedded so mistakes are repeated...).

I notice the difference in my business when I'm attending to each of the seasons intentionally. My default is to be in Spring; I love planning, mapping new options, thinking about new ideas. I also love the snuggly, quiet energy of Winter. I'd happily miss out on the detail orientation of Autumn and the go-for-it visibility of Summer. My business has thrived when I've paid consistent, regular attention to the architecture, systems and structures in my business (Autumn), and when I've leaned into the energy of visibility (Summer).

There are multiple benefits of living seasonally and cyclically:

- Less push, less hustle, less grind
- Accessing flow, balance and building resilience
- Balancing our '*on*' and '*out*ward' facing energy with our '*in*ward' energy
- Making our change-making contribution in a more sustainable way.

Use Table 2.1 and the following reflection point to identify how you can use the seasons for your life and change-making work.

TABLE 2.1 Honouring the seasons

If you're in...	Can you give attention to...	Your ideas to honour this season in your change making
Spring	Exploring new beginnings, new opportunities, mapping out your ideas and plans, allowing small ideas to begin to flourish	
Summer	Visibility, promotion, reaching out to new connections, seeking out collaborations. Also play, enjoying relationships and having fun	
Autumn	Finishing off key projects, dotting 'i's and crossing 't's, culmination, reviewing learning	
Winter	Rest, evaluation, intuitive and creative thinking, healing	

REFLECTION POINT

1   Which season needs more attention from you?

2   Are there new skills to learn, to maximize the value of this season?

3   What shifts, if you embrace the season that you're in?

4   How can you honour this season? Even 10% more?

5   What's the *gift* for you from this season?

And now step back to look at your answers above:

What are your insights?

What do you notice from this exercise? What do you want to shift?

....
....
....
....
....

Unwind rewind: chapter summary

In this chapter we've shared some different lenses to go deeper into the self-discovery and reality-check question 'Where am I?'

In Part 1 we explored your inner dialogue, the conversation of your thoughts inside your head, as a resource for you! You can befriend your inner critic, you can tune into the voice of your inner wisdom and extend your growth mindset. We explored how to snap out of rumination into healthy reflection. These are foundational wellbeing pieces for your change-making leadership.

In Part 2 you connected with a sense of who you are as a change-making leader, exploring your leadership identity through the lens of the intersectional identity map.

In Part 3 we looked at how the seasons of Spring, Summer, Autumn and Winter can bring rich insights, and the benefits of living seasonally and cyclically for our change making.

We've covered the power practices of 'Hearing your inner wisdom', 'Dialling down your inner critic' and 'Shifting out of rumination'.

In Chapter 3 we're strengthening your resilience!

UNWIND REWIND

What's most important for you from this chapter?

What did you learn about your inner dialogue and growth mindset?

What does your inner wisdom want you to know?

What season of life are you in (Spring, Summer, Autumn, Winter)?

Think about your current workplace. What season is the default season in your organizational culture?

What power practices will you experiment with to build your healthy mental habits?

Record your thoughts in your **progress tracker** or your journal.

On resilience

I keep my goals clear in my mind and reviewing them often helps me stay focused day to day.

On collaboration and sisterhood

I try to look at things as 'a rising tide lifts all boats' which really has shaped how I lift others up and support them, even if they do similar business to me. I lift others up, amplifying their voices, and give those who aren't sure what to say yet an option to explore, speak and share, through my everyday work, as well as my podcast and through my socials.

CHANGE MAKER INTERVIEW   Lauren Currie

Lauren Currie OBE *is the founder of UPFRONT, an organization on a mission to change confidence, visibility and power for women and marginalized communities. Lauren is a keynote speaker, chairperson of leading maternity discrimination organization Pregnant Then Screwed and has been recognized as a woman changing the world by* Elle *magazine and as one of the top businesswomen under 35 by* Management Today. *In 2017, she was awarded an OBE for her services to design and diversity. She grew up in Scotland and now lives in Stockholm with her family.*

I asked Lauren about how we can discover our sense of purpose, navigating barriers, bias and opposition in her change-making work and what it means to 'get a seat at the table'.

I'm a change maker because it's who I am. I don't have any other choice.

Women are not born feeling less than. The world teaches us to believe we are less than. This is the reality I'm working to change. I'm not here to change women. I'm here to change the effect the patriarchy has on us. Women are fine. It's the sh*t that's thrown at us that needs to change.

I started my first business when I was 23. I felt like an outsider. As my power and influence grew, I was invited into traditionally powerful spaces where I was often the only woman and usually the youngest person in the room. This led me to question how other women are treated and how other women feel.

Activism and intersectionality are the key tenets of my work. My focus is on collective progress over individual progress; discomfort over comfort. My leadership style is not one where I light up the room; it's one where I encourage everyone in the room to turn their own lights on.

I've had a little insight into what it's like to move through the world as part of an oppressed population and, as much as I find this extremely frustrating and difficult at times, I am a white woman. I am never judged or treated differently because of the colour of my skin.

I'm only just starting to learn how little I really understand.

I experience bias every day. I've faced intense ageism and sexism. I'm constantly held back and blocked by old power – white men protesting the status quo. It's exhausting but as a white, non-disabled, straight woman I have immense privilege. I navigate it in a few different ways:

1   as an opportunity to educate myself on how to respond to prejudice;

2   as an opportunity to be a good ally and educate myself on the depth and extent of my privilege;

3   by turning my rage into action which fuels my work.

When I experience opposition, I try to focus on where it's coming from. I try to be kind, diplomatic and self-compassionate. I remind myself of the impact I'm having. That the results are worth this sacrifice. That being an ally should cost me. I must be prepared to invest.

There's no one future of work, only multiple futures of work. I think it looks feminist in its values, practices and behaviour. It looks intersectional, genuinely diverse, inclusive and fair. We need universal basic income and universal healthcare. No billionaires, no prisons and no meat eaters. The latter is what's necessary for our planet: it has to be vegan and sustainable.

CHAPTER THREE

Change-making resilience

'How are you?'

Do the best you can until you know better, then when you know better, do better. MAYA ANGELOU

When did you last take a nap?

No seriously, when did you last decide to have a sleep, or rest, in the day, just because?

When you're involved in change-making work and leadership, it's fulfilling, but it's also draining. You care passionately but you can also feel fatigued, exhausted and burned out. Disappointment and resentment can fester.

Whether or not you're choosing to work explicitly in social change spaces, the Covid-19 pandemic has impacted all of us, although experienced differently depending on our access to power and privilege. We've all been through unprecedented pressure and strain, the fear, losses and grief associated with the pandemic itself, alongside the uncertainty of closures, lockdowns, economic and political repercussions. There's been unrelenting political turmoil, as well as global consciousness-raising around social injustice, racial inequities, environmental and climate disasters. In response to this we can cycle through fogginess, numbness, exhaustion. All these responses are part of being human. The cumulative exhaustion is real.[1]

Wherever your start-point, as change makers, as leaders, as humans (!) it's so important that we prioritize our own resilience, sustainability and wellbeing.

In this chapter we're going to:

- reframe our concept of time and bust the busy-ness myth;
- shift from a focus on managing time to managing energy;
- track our energy and our seasons, continuing to reset our central nervous system;
- create our own resilience map;
- experience a thriving visualization;
- set our intentions and craft a morning routine.

> Resilience is our ability to bounce back from hardship, adversity and challenge. It's the mental, physical, emotional, relational and ecological strength we build to sustain us and enable us to recover from knocks.

The tyranny of busy and shifting our concept of time from linear/lack to stretchy/abundant

We know we need to care for ourselves, to enable ourselves to be sustainable, and we mostly know how to do that: eat nutritious food, sleep, exercise, hydrate, take regular breaks and so on… but there's often a gap between *knowing* the best thing for ourselves, and actually *doing* it![2]

Our **beliefs about self-care** leak out in our language. Have you ever said:

'I'm so busy.'
'I'm overwhelmed.'

Busy can be a badge of honour in our culture. As such, books, research and thought leadership about resilience can emphasize productivity, time management, maximizing your ability to keep going, or characterize self-care as a reward for productivity, or a means to enable you to 'get back to' your peak productivity. Society tells us we don't need deep rest, we just need enough to help us to keep going and stay productive. 'I'm so busy' can be a default setting; it creates a culture, it becomes the norm. We're socialized so strongly into this model of what a 'good worker' and a 'good citizen' looks like. We don't always see it – our bodies often feel it before we cognitively recognize it!

Burnout is a *symptom*.

Burnout is based in a masculinized, ableist, ageist, capitalist system, where our value is what our human bodies can produce and consume. This generates rushing, overwhelm and burnout. It's also based around *lack* and keeping us compliant as workers in the system.

I find the term 'resilience' a tricky idea as it's used within the highly competitive sectors I've worked within to place the responsibility for 'not coping' with unrealistic demands and workload on the individual, rather than challenging institutions to create a more achievable workload. High levels of mental ill-health are the outcomes of unrealistic pressures on employees. I'd prefer the discourse to be around 'realistic institutional expectations' rather than 'individual employee resilience'. (Fiona Cuthill)

I talked with Dr Leyla Hussein, psychotherapist, international lecturer and award-winning campaigner, global expert on FGM, founder of The Dahlia Project, Director for Africa-led Movement to End FGM and (first Black woman to be) Rector of the University of St Andrews. Leyla shared her experiences of burnout, being intentional about our wellbeing, and how she thrives and stays sustainable inside her workspaces:

Human beings, particularly those working in social justice, humanitarian sectors, and also entrepreneurs, people who're really passionate about their work... they start with good intentions, the subjects we pick to work with are very close to us – that's why we recognize it so well. But the other spectrum of that is you're experiencing triggers, you're reliving traumas again. For example, interviewing women (who've experienced violence) in Congo, the woman in London may also be triggered and she also needs support. We don't have spaces for that.

In the work I choose to do – I'm not hearing great stories! and I'm working on something I've experienced myself, so I'm constantly reliving my own trauma. So, I'm very, very intentional about my own wellbeing.

We have to be intentional about it – it's not embedded into our systems.

When women tell me that focusing on wellbeing can feel selfish, I tell them about conditioning. We need to decolonize our state of mind that when we prioritize ourselves we are selfish. Especially mothers – you'd be a better mother when you take care of yourself first. Put on the mask first before you put it on others – that analogy is so true. As women, we're conditioned to this idea we're saving everybody else, we're sacrificing ourselves. We're expected to hold the whole of society but when it comes to our own self-care, we're called selfish.

Why would you being well and happy and having pleasure be selfish? When you're in that good state of mind, it trickles to all the rest of your life. I know I'm a better colleague when I take care of myself and I'm intentional about my self-care.

Our **beliefs about time** leak out in our language. Have you ever said:

'I don't have enough time.'
'I carved out some time.'
'We're running out of time.'

Often resilience is shaped as a fight against time, a way to keep ourselves strong in the face of onslaughts of expectations from our culture. If we're in a mindset of *lack* around time, then there's never enough, we're always going to be pressed and pressurized. We're socialized to believe that we're living in lack. That we need to *be more*, that we need to *acquire more stuff* and that we need to *do more*, to be worthy. The world is full of money; the issue is not lack of money, the issue is distribution and injustice, which means resources are not distributed equitably.

When we loosen up our concept of time from solely linear and something based in lack, we open up new opportunities for living abundantly. Sometimes we experience time as passing 'in a flash', sometimes 'it drags', sometimes it 'stands still'. When we're in a flow state we're deeply absorbed in the present moment. Time can actually be experienced as quite 'stretchy'[3] and yet the present is all we have, recurring, now.[4]

I encourage you to shift to a concept of time as seasonal, cyclical, re-occurring in the *present*. The power practices in this book invite us to return to our bodies, return to the present moment of *now*, tune into our energy moment-to-moment. This is how we can experience presence, spaciousness, abundance, even if our schedule is full and our to-do list is bulging.

Let's experiment with this, using the following reflection point.

REFLECTION POINT

Instead of saying

'I don't have enough time'

Try saying

'There's enough time and space for all the things today'

OR

'I have enough xxx (time, resources, money – whatever you currently see in lack) to get me to the next step'

What does this shift for you? What starts to loosen up?!

....
....
....
....
....

Do you see how our chapter on resilience can't just be about our personal health and wellbeing (as important as that is), but it's so much about the system! I encourage you to identify your own knowing–doing gap and explore what beliefs might be running for you in the gap. Use the power practices from Chapters 1 and 2 to listen to your inner dialogue. What are the socialized and conditioned beliefs you're holding, about rest, productivity, wellbeing, time and pleasure, that you can reclaim and heal? Use the following reflection point to help you.

REFLECTION POINT

Do I believe I deserve rest?

Do I have to earn it?

Do I believe I deserve pleasure?

....
....
....
....
....

Let us practice normalizing rest and self-care as a necessary part of our human experience and stop using them as mere tools to support (toxic) productivity. (Tamu Thomas)

When we shift our mindset around time, we can start to manage our *energy*.

From managing time to managing energy – check in with your battery

I think about resilience as *energy* – your intention/attention/blood, sweat and tears of your life!

Let's use the analogy of a battery. You can gauge your own energy levels and check inwards to see how 'topped up' your battery is, at any time of day or night.

EXERCISE   Battery check-in

Check in with yourself right now. Think about yourself as a battery.

Close your eyes if you like. Take a deep breath.

Check in with your body, mind, emotions (and spirit if that's in your awareness).

What's your energy level? How topped up is your battery right now? Are you at 80%, 63%, 47%, 20%?

If your energy's high right now, can you recognize what's contributing to this? How can you make the most of this high energy?

> If your energy's low, can you recognize what's contributing to this? Can you tune into what you may need to help you top up? Do you need to rest or have a nap? Come off your screens? Breathe some fresh air? Eat something nutritious? Drink some water? Call a friend?

Tracking your energy

I encourage you to check in with your energy like this, throughout the day, and *just notice*. Keep track using the energy tracker shown in Table 3.1 for a few days, then use the prompts below to have a look back. You can download a full week's trackers in the bonus resources at my site.[5]

What do you notice?

You're looking for patterns. You may already think 'I know I'm a morning person' or 'it takes me a while to get going', but allow your mind to be open to fresh thinking here. Your body may have some new and additional data to share with you.

Daily bio-rhythms

What do you notice about how your **energy ebbs and flows** at different times of day? When is your energy at its highest? Lowest? Mid-point? Are you up with the lark? Are you a night owl? Do you have an energy dip early afternoon? If I gave you permission to take a nap uninterrupted at any time of the day (and I promise you wouldn't wake up groggy!), when would you choose? What does this tell you about your flow of energy through a day?

TABLE 3.1 Your energy tracker

Day 1

Time of day	Battery check-in – what's the %?	What am I doing/who am I with?	Anything else I notice about my energy

Do you start to notice the interplay of your nutrition, rest, exercise and hydration and those micro-moments of choice? What happens to your energy if you choose to drink more water or more coffee? What happens if you choose to eat a biscuit, or some nuts, or an apple?

Let's look next at your **task-focused energy**. What kinds of things are you doing when your energy is at its highest? Lowest? Again, you're looking for patterns.

Now let's look at the **impact of different relationships on your energy**. Who were you with when your energy was highest? Lowest? Who peps you up and tends to boost your energy? Who drains your energy?

This is about tuning in to your body in a more intimate way and listening to your needs. Again, to reiterate, our culture tells us we're most valuable when we 'push through', which means ignoring or denying any energy dips. This practice is about noticing the ebbs and flows (so that you can embrace them!).

What do you notice as you step back from this data? What does this tell you?

Is there anything you're going to shift up and experiment with over the next few days, in order to maximize your daily energy?

So many of my clients had *never* done this before we worked together, and the data they receive from their own bodies is *dynamite* for their leadership going forward. Keep going with this tracking and noticing exercise for a few days in a row. You may not want to jump straight into conclusive action! What do you want to stay curious about and track some more? In Chapter 4 we'll be coming back to this energy tracker as you work on a plan to maximize your energy.

A gentle reminder that this is not an opportunity to beat yourself up or get stuck in 'oughts' or 'shoulds' or the rumination loops we discussed in Chapter 2 of 'I wish I'd...'. Remember we looked at seasons and the concept of living and working in cycles, rather than purely linear and 'always on'. The intention and purpose with this exercise is to spot opportunities for your learning and growth. We can choose a growth mindset, start fresh each day, with compassion for ourselves here.

Weekly rhythms

As you complete your daily energy tracker for at least a week and then into several weeks, what do you notice about your *weekly* energy and rhythms? I have clients who bounce out of bed on a Monday morning raring to start the week, and then are flagging by Friday; I've others who drag themselves into work on Mondays and 'warm up' as the week progresses. I notice I can tend to have a 'push through till the weekend' mentality. If I actually check in with my weekly rhythms, I often find myself lower in energy during Wednesday and Thursday afternoons, and can be quite energized again by Friday (if I've rested mid-week, rather than 'pushed through'!). What about you?

Do you build in **weekly rest**? A regular time for a halt to pushing and productivity? It's a space for recuperation, physical rest, emotional processing, replenishment of soul and spirit. Most ancient wisdom and faith traditions build spaces of rest into their regular patterns. The rest in your week is the Winter part of the cycle, where the ground lies fallow, the seeds are under the ground, it appears as if nothing's growing, and yet the deep work of restoration, healing, preparation is happening under the ground. Whether or not connection with the divine is your thing, I encourage you to consider weekly rest as a sacred and essential ingredient in the mix of your life.

We can see how choice-filled rest becomes radically coun-ter-cultural.[6] We can align with Tamu Thomas who asserts that: 'I refuse to allow what takes care of me and what makes me feel good be a rebellion, nor be a resistance. It's mine, it's purely for me, because that's what I need. If it causes ripples elsewhere, that's fine.'

Monthly rhythms – do you track your periods?

When you've tracked your days for a number of weeks, then into months, you may start to notice that your energy flows in different ways at different stages of your monthly cycle (if you're bleeding). You may notice an energized outward focus during your ovulation phase (Summer), and more focused detail orientation during your luteal phase (Autumn – the longest phase of the cycle). You may notice a need for rest and quiet during your menstruation phase (Winter), and a boost of energy as you enter into follicular stage (Spring).[7]

STORY Tracking my cycle

When I'm in my menstrual phase, with the energy of Winter, I need earlier nights, less screen time, more open space, more sofa time, so I can maximize the intuitive and creative-thinking opportunities present for me in that phase, and so I can prevent myself getting tired out. In the past (most of my life, being honest!), I learned and internalized the message that periods weren't to stop me doing anything. This message has the positive intent of not stigmatizing girls or women on their bleed, but it also works to silence, minimize and deny the possibility that our bodies may have different needs at different times of the month. I'd essentially ignore my body, not listen to the clues that I needed extra rest, 'push through', make efforts to hide the bleed, and otherwise carry on in the linear A–Z workplace mentality.

Now that we've busted a few myths and reframed our concepts around time and energy, let's go deeper with how we can live more cyclically, reset our central nervous systems and create our own resilience map!

Your holistic resilience map

I think about resilience holistically, with a model that interconnects mental, physical, emotional, relational, locational and spiritual wellbeing. These are the different aspects that make up and boost our battery energy, the *basics* where we can give attention to ensure we're building healthy foundations for our life and change-making leadership.

The circles in the resilience map (Figure 3.1) indicate the areas where we've power and agency (back to Principle 2 from our Introduction). We can also add 'ancestral' to acknowledge that we carry in our bodies and our heritage trauma that we and our ancestors experienced. We can add 'environmental' and 'societal' wellbeing to acknowledge how the wider context of our lives, and the systems we move around and within, impact our energy, and that we also influence.

Have a look at the resilience map and at Table 3.2, and identify which areas need more attention.

FIGURE 3.1   Resilience map

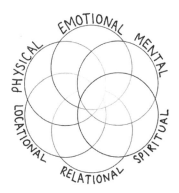

TABLE 3.2 Your resilience map

Aspect of your battery energy	Mental	Emotional	Relational	Physical	Spiritual	Locational
Activities to top up your energy	Nurturing healthy mental habits to counteract negativity bias and minimize thinking errors	Doing things every day that you love	Healthy loving relationships	Hydration	Feeling part of something bigger than yourself	Declutter[8]
	Resetting your central nervous system to shift out of threat response	Feeling the way you want to feel	Fun and friendship	Nutrition	Nurturing your beliefs	Create a space that feels lovely for you (even a small corner)
		Choosing and taking decisions for your own life	Intimacy, pleasure and connection	Sleep	Connecting to your values and what's most important to you	Use colours, scents, fabrics, accessories you love and that bring you joy
		Gratitude power practice	Forgiveness and grace	Movement	Living in alignment with your	Mix up your work location
		Beauty spotting power practice	Letting go of regrets and grudges	Fresh air and time in nature		Get into nature

All the power practices throughout this book cover one or more of these areas, some of them dialling up multiple areas for a mega-boost! As the circles are interlocking and these parts of you are all interconnected, by giving some intentional energy to one area, there's a positive knock-on effect to the other areas. For example, we know that taking a regular brisk walk has physical fitness benefits, and we know it also positively impacts emotional and mental wellbeing. Listening to music has multiple emotional, mental, spiritual, even relational benefits. The beauty-spotting and gratitude power practices give you a boost of feel-good energy that'll impact you mentally, emotionally and physically. The intention-setting power practice is a boost for your mental, emotional and spiritual wellbeing, and it also impacts relationally.

Your resilience map

See Table 3.2.

So much of this we know, right? But what areas can *you* dial up today? Use the following reflection point to help you.

REFLECTION POINT

Which areas of the resilience map are topped up for you? Which of these areas feel depleted?

Where can you give some specific attention to top up your energy battery?

....
....
....
....
....

Micro-resilience

Sometimes when we check in with our battery, it may be only a very small shift that's needed to boost our energy and wellbeing, in that moment. Here's an opportunity for a mini top-up, a moment of micro-resilience, and the research suggests that frequent energy top-ups are significantly better for us than fewer longer breaks.[9] This is great news! In your busy change-maker life, you don't need to build in *big* resilience moments. Take all the micro-moments you can!

As an example, I notice I've been typing here in a very focused way, and when I look away from my screen for a moment, I realize my eyes are strained, my neck and shoulders feel stiff. I hadn't noticed this, but now I'm checking in I notice my battery's around 40 per cent. I have a choice point here. This is a micro-resilience, mini top-up moment! I can choose to 'push through', or I can choose to 'top up' my battery. I step away from my desk, do a stretch up and down, side to side, touch my toes. I look out the window to shift my focal length. I sit back down, take a sip of my peppermint tea, relishing the warmth and the flavour for a moment, rather than slurping it while typing.

I encourage you to become attuned to these really small shifts when you check in with your battery. The key is to s-t-r-e-t-c-h out the moment, embody it, relish it. These moments of micro-resilience develop new neural pathways and lock in positive feelings and resonances from your day. Remember we're building small consistent practices here that make a difference over time. We're connecting with positive emotion, relishing pleasure and joy, resetting our central nervous systems. We're shifting out of a threat response into a relaxation response, which if you recall from Chapter 1 enables our brains to function with fewer *thinking errors* aka *bias*. It's essential for our functioning as change-making leaders that we're practised at accessing our micro-resilience moments!

There are multiple opportunities for micro-resilience and battery top-ups throughout your day. Think of all the **transition times**: in-between meetings, even when we're working from home and it's all on Zoom or Teams! There are very small 'in-between' spaces. Take a pee, make a drink, take a stretch, a yoga flow, run up and down the stairs, do some star-jumps or burpees if you're able, put on some high-energy music for a boost or some chilled music for a relaxation break, come back to your intentions (see below).

The purpose here is to change your state, boost your energy, top up your battery. Use the following reflection point to think about the opportunities available to you.

REFLECTION POINT

Where are your opportunities for micro-resilience moments today?

How can you relish these moments even more?

....
....
....
....
....

You at your best – thriving visualization

We're going to run a thriving visualization, where you'll identify your best future self and see what insights she gives you! Visualization is another way for you to listen to your inner wisdom, inviting your imagination and intuition to speak. The visualization can become a touchpoint for you, to help you see what's possible for you in your life and change-making work, when you're at your best.[10]

As this is a closed-eye exercise, I suggest you read it through a few times before attempting it, or download the audio version from the book bonuses at my site, or ask a friend you trust to lead you through this process – you can then switch and do it for them![11]

POWER PRACTICE   Thriving visualization

Close your eyes.

Tune into your breath.

Deepen your inhale, imagine breathing into the bottom of your lungs, to the middle of your backbone.

Lengthen out your exhale, you can even sigh out, or say or imagine the word 'release' as you exhale.

Notice that many thoughts may come into your awareness… that's normal and fine; just gently bring your attention back to your breath, every time you notice a thought in your mind.

Now bring to your imagination an image of yourself in the future.

---

3 **What's one thing I want to *progress*?** When we think about our big goals they can feel overwhelming or hard to break down into day-to day tasks. We procrastinate the important stuff because we can't complete it in the time we've available to us. The word 'progress' is key here. We can *choose one thing* that's a small move, that'll take us *towards* our bigger goals. If you just have 20 minutes today, what small thing can you do in that time slot that'll progress you towards your most important life and work goals? By the way, if for a few days in a row you take small steps towards your goals, guess what, you're on your way to making significant progress! Go back to your energy tracker where you tracked your daily, weekly, monthly, rhythms. When are you at your best energy for progressing important (small) tasks? That's when to do it! This will link up in Chapter 5 when you identify your goals and change-making focus.

Kick-start your morning routine

I read recently about the morning routine of a particularly well-known entrepreneur. It totally turned me off. He wakes up, hangs upside down for 20 minutes, reads spiritual texts for 30 minutes, does cardio exercise for 20 minutes, swims in a cold pool for 20 minutes, then drinks ginger tea and journals for 20 minutes and on and on, blah blah and I've already turned the page…. And yes, if you're curious, he's a single male, with no other caring responsibilities! If you can make all that work for you each morning, *good for you.*

We all have a different mix in our days and who, if anyone, we're sharing our morning space with. So, make your morning routine fit for you, your stage of life and your lifestyle.

The *minimum* for me is:

1 Make my bed.
2 Move my body.
3 Set my intentions.

And I can do this even if I'm in a rush, if we've all slept in, if I'm waking up with a jumble of kids in my bed. If I've more space (for me, that's on those work days when I'm away from family and wake up in a hotel room, blissfully alone!) then I extend each piece.

1 **Make your bed.** If you don't already do this (no judgement!), trust me, it makes a massive difference. See these few moments as a space for you to *create* and *complete*. When my kids were small and my house was permanently very, very messy (actually nothing's changed now that they're teenagers, who am I trying to kid!), I knew this could be the only space in my home that would remain the way I made it, when I returned to it later. When so much of my daily consulting and coaching work can be quite complex and 'ongoing', with no clear end points, making my bed is a satisfying moment of accomplishment in my day and research shows it has many benefits.[12]

2 **Move your body.** However you like to do it best, and however you're able. For some, that's a morning run or swim, for others it's a five-minute yoga flow or simple

stretch-out. Connect this to the seasons we talked about in Chapter 2. If my energy's in Summer (and if it's actually Summer when the mornings are super light) then I'll bounce out of bed to walk up the hill close to my home, yoga stretch at the top and run back down. When my energy's Spring then my body is more up for a short HIIT (high-intensity interval training) or dance workout. When my energy's more like Winter or Autumn, then stretches and a short yoga flow are enough! Match your exercise for the best fit with your seasonal energy.

3 **Set your intentions.** As intention setting becomes a daily habit, you start to experience its magic and power. See 'Setting your intentions' above.

Make your morning routine work for you, but *do it*!

Extending your morning routine

Look back at your resilience map to see what you wanted to dial up – how can you build this into your morning routine? For example, on nutrition, do you want to start taking supplements or adding a piece of fruit or a smoothie to your breakfast? Do you want to add movement? Do you want to add some prayer, meditation or gratitude? Don't overcommit, or it may feel too cumbersome on your fuller days. Start small and give it a try for a few days in a row; we're building habits here.

Once your morning routine is established, enjoy the rhythm and ease of it. You'll get to a stage where you're unconsciously competent (you don't even really have to think about it) and it just flows.

When you're ready, you can mix it up again, or add another element, to stay fresh.

NB: I'm doing the three essentials above *before* I reach for my phone and it's been a *game-changer* for my wellbeing. It takes discipline, but it means I'm feeling how I want to feel before I allow anyone else's urgency or drama to capture my attention.

REFLECTION POINT

- What does your morning routine consist of at the moment?
- What else are you going to experiment with?
- What small shifts from your resilience map are you going to build into your morning routine?

....
....
....
....
....

Unwind rewind: chapter summary

In Chapter 3 we've covered:

- A reminder that your wellbeing and resilience is important in and of itself; you don't need to earn it or deserve it. *And* it's an essential building block as you step up in your leadership.
- You already know a lot about your own resilience and what sustains it – now you can *do* those specific things

CHANGE MAKER INTERVIEW   Sonya Barlow

Sonya Barlow is an award-winning entrepreneur, founder and CEO of Like Minded Females Network, TEDx speaker, business lecturer, radio host and diversity consultant. She was recently recognized as a LinkedIn Changemaker as advocate of Gender Equality and Diversity.

I talked with Sonya about her change making in the tech and entrepreneurship worlds, her daily habits to stay resilient, finding out her change-making contribution, building collaboration and how she navigates barriers.

I'm a change maker because I've learned to love myself, voice and opinion – which influences all my decisions. I've pledged to create an impact around social good, especially female empowerment and inclusive cultures. My purpose is to enable inclusive cultures, build strong communities and remind people that they have their best version of themselves inside of them.

It makes me angry and determined when I hear stories of people not achieving their potential based on barriers, either through unconscious bias or by lack of understanding from companies. There are many reasons why talented ethnic minority individuals leave the technology industry or business industry or can't move up.

On daily habits

One of my practices to stay resilient is always to think: 'the worst thing I can do is not try'. I'd rather do my best and fail, than regret not taking that chance.

In my journey as an entrepreneur, I've failed more than I've succeeded. By asking myself, 'What did I do wrong and what can I do differently next time?' I've grown both professionally and personally.

I know that I'm a procrastinator, so I make lists to tick off daily, including house and personal stuff. That way, I can shuffle from one to another when something doesn't work and at least get something done. It's a term I've coined: 'productive procrastination'.

On finding our change-making contribution

The first step is finding something, a cause or a problem you want to solve, that you feel passionate about. Sometimes it will come easy, and other times you'll find it during your professional life. This would be a skill or strength of yours that others make fun of, but you know that is your muscle.

Talking to people from backgrounds different from yours also helps you broaden your mindset and helps you find your unique voice and potential contribution.

I believe that discovering your purpose can be a lifelong endeavour. Even if you find your passion, you'll always continue to identify new ways to make a change.

On building collaboration and partnership support into our ecosystems

I'd have never been able to build and grow LMF Network if it wasn't for the fantastic work done by our volunteers. They're also a support system and cheerleading squad, especially during the hard days.

My advice is to find and meet like-minded individuals who share your vision of change, and then nurture those relationships. It could be as simple as keeping in touch, giving and asking for advice, or even inviting them to collaborate with you on a project.

On navigating barriers and bias

When I worked in the tech industry, before being a full-time entrepreneur, I experienced workplace bullying and toxicity.

I won't lie – it was hard at the beginning. No-one teaches you how to deal with bad managers or toxic workplaces or even handle reticent clients. These experiences can impact your confidence in yourself and your work.

From senior managers mispronouncing my name to seeing women being shot down at meetings; I also met resistance when I tried to push for diversity and inclusion initiatives, because management said they didn't generate revenue and were unnecessary.

These kinds of experiences are still happening in many organizations. I learned to navigate them better and also do something to change it. I've learned to negotiate and find common ground between two – sometimes – opposing views. The key is not losing sight of the end goals and always looking for win–win solutions to any situation.

Other times it's a matter of knowing your worth and stepping away when things don't align. Learning how to say no is just as important as knowing when to say yes.

As a social entrepreneur, I've met incredible and supportive people who're also seeking to make changes to the world of work.

On dealing with opposition to your change-making work

I deal with it in three ways, at different levels. First, I strive to be a thought leader on the diversity and inclusion agenda. Second, I work on educating companies on why diversity, inclusion and equity initiatives are essential and how they can implement them effectively. Finally, I seek to empower others to start these conversations in their own networks, whether at universities or workplaces.

What do you see is the future of work, such that it meets people's needs?

The future of work should be where inclusive environments are the standard, not the exception. Diversity, inclusion and equity should be part of all companies' core business practices and not just 'nice to have' initiatives.

The other element is flexible working. Covid-19 taught us that most jobs can be done from home, and organizations should have work from home policies so people can have a work–life balance or even accommodate their responsibilities if they are carers.

CHAPTER FOUR

Change-making plan

'What do you want?'

OK, now we've got these foundations of self-awareness (Chapters 1 and 2) and self-resilience (Chapter 3) in place, we're going to dig deeper throughout the rest of this book into your leadership context and your change-making focus. You met your best future self in Chapter 3, living your best life, making your dream difference. This chapter goes deeper on helping bring her into your reality *now*.

This chapter is all about tapping into your desires, what you actually want (and don't want) for your life, and how this can powerfully help ground and guide you as a change-making leader. You'll be listening to yourself, getting to know yourself better and trusting yourself more deeply.

When we do this, we access our inner wisdom, find our North Star through listening to our own intuition, and keep going towards our goals. We're unlearning and relearning our conditioning that (particularly as women and if we hold other marginalized identities) we're not safe to identify or articulate our desires, and that our safety is secured through pleasing others and fitting in.[1]

We'll also explore the contribution you want to make, from a place of joy, connection and deep 'yes', rather than being driven by others' expectations.

These skills are foundational for you in your change-making leadership inside your workplace. We're going to start by exploring our desires with the question 'what do you want?' We then unpack how we can hear our desires and start to articulate them, using a model called Ikigai to help us do that. We'll also explore our joy, our jealousy and our deep 'yes'. This chapter will bring you a massive dose of positivity!

Tapping into your desires

What do you desire?

What do you want?

What do you *really* want?

It seems like a really basic question, but it's a dangerous one.

If you're used to prioritizing others' needs, whether in your home, workplace or both, you may be unaccustomed to being asked, and answering, this question. As girls and young women (in Western society), we're not usually socialized to connect with our desires and answer this question for ourselves. Our initial answers may reflect others' expectations of us. We're socialized and taught to not express ourselves, to second guess, holding back on our ideas, opinions and perspectives.[2] In workplaces we're talked over, interrupted, mansplained.[3] For some of us with marginalized identities, or living in particularly challenging home circumstances, it may not be or feel safe to identify and articulate our desires.

To be clear, when I ask you 'what do you want?', I'm not asking about materialistic things. I'm asking about the *quality of your life*, what do you want to *feel*, what *difference* do you want to make, what *legacy* do you want to leave, what's *most important* to you, and how can you access even more of that? 'What do I want?' connects us with something bigger than ourselves, taking us beyond the confines of our individual lives. 'What do I want?' connects us with our deepest needs, our pleasure, our drives and motivations, our unique perspectives, insights and opinions, our source energy, the expression of our own humanity.

Connecting with your desires is how you find your purpose and North Star, that guiding light. Gaining clarity of what we want guides the contribution we want to make, rather than living a life that meets others' expectations or lives someone else's dream. Our desires lead us to connection and solidarity with others – it's how we find our people. Expressing your desires is part of how you discover your voice, find out what you really think about things, start to show up, speak up and step up!

Clarity and focus in our lives are key ingredients of happiness and wellbeing.[4] When we're clear what we're saying 'yes' to, our 'no's become a lot easier. We can then more easily hold boundaries, ask for help and receive support. We're less likely to burn out when our work comes from that place of joy, desire and 'yes'. We become more sustainable when we're connected with our desires.[5]

As we're unlearning our internal conditioning, we're modelling, giving permission and opening doors for others, unleashing a positive ripple effect.

This is radical stuff! Connecting with our desires is a key piece of unlearning as women in the world! This is part of how we dismantle the patriarchy and build our foundations to 'chip away at the wall'. As career coach Jaz Broughton reminds us, 'your job is to find yourself and then become more of her. Don't let anyone or anything get in the way of that.'

What do you actually want for your life?

We've established why it's foundational to our change-making leadership that we learn to tap into our desires. It's a privilege to dream bigger and visualize a better world for yourself and those around you. It's a responsibility to tune into that and then to act on it. So, let's practise!

Go back to your thriving visualization from Chapter 3 and your inner wisdom power practice in Chapter 2. What did your imagination and your inner wisdom show you?

What's the fabric of that dream – living your best life, making your dream difference? You may feel you've a very long way to go, but getting the detail for yourself is key. You don't want to be living someone else's dream.

This guided power practice builds out the detail for you from the thriving visualization we did together in Chapter 3.

You can do this as a closed-eye exercise (read it through first!) or write down the answers to the questions in your journal; try to 'free write' rather than censor yourself – you can make sense of it later.

EXERCISE   What do I want?

Find an undisturbed space, close your eyes for a moment.

Connect with your breath and access your relaxation response (see Chapter 1 to refresh yourself with this).

Invite your inner wisdom to show up and speak with you clearly.

Choose to be open and receptive.

Work your way through these prompts:

What do I want?

Wait patiently.

Ask again, what do I want…?

Then ask:

What do I really want…?

How do I want to feel?

What does it feel like, when I feel like that? (Allow more words to surface.)

What are the thoughts that come up for me, when I feel like that? (Just notice, no judgement.)

Then you can enquire: what do I want in my:

○   work and career
○   business

- ○ leadership and change-making
- ○ money and finances
- ○ relationships
- ○ family and parenting
- ○ sex life and love life?

What do I want for my:

- ○ body and physical health
- ○ psychological health and wellbeing
- ○ spiritual and emotional health
- ○ friendships and community?

What contribution do I want to make?

What change do I want to be part of?

What do I definitely *not* want?

Try not to censor what your mind gives you, and listen in to all that your imagination wants to show you.

You can pause at any time. You can come back at any time.

If you've been practising hearing your inner critic and inner wisdom, you can distinguish their distinctive voices. Notice if permission, constraint or a critical voice comes up, and note down what it's saying.

NB: This exercise can be a deep reflection. You may choose to work through what comes up for you with a therapist, coach or trusted friend.

If you'd like to stretch yourself a little further, you can take this next step.

EXERCISE Next-level desires

If I receive all that I want… and if it's done, present, real and already here…

What's next… what is the next level of what I want…?

What else is possible?

What do I want my contribution to be *now*?

What else is in my heart?

Write it down! You can come back to make sense of it later.

You may see a bigger sense of what you'd like for your life, the impact you want to have. You may only get the next few steps; you don't always see the full picture. Sometimes the desires we have are latent for a while and then burst out.

STORY Tapping into our desires

It's December 2017 and some new creativity and possibility have been bubbling inside me for a while. I know I want to write, to create, to express… but I don't know what I want to say. I certainly don't know how I'll say it.

I'm ill over the Christmas holidays – a blur of fever while my relatives forage for their own dinners. I ask myself the question: what do I want? I wake up with clarity several days later, sickness passed, with a calm clear voice inside me: 'who are you waiting for, to give you permission?'

I realize I'm waiting for someone, outside of myself, to give me permission to go for it (whatever 'it' is!).

Whose permission am I waiting for: My partner? My brother? My Dad? God?! (Notice the male authority figures who hold positions of influence for me at this stage of my life.)

That evening after the kids are in bed, I make snacks, dig out my laptop, and cosy up to the log burner.

I write 3000 words non-stop. They flow out of me. It's like a cork flying out of a bottle. And the words continue to flow.

Very soon afterwards I meet the amazing woman who'd become my business partner for the following three years. We write and create together. We set up a new venture and scale a business to multiple six figures. From this initial expressing of myself flowed collaboration, creation and impact.

More joy

When we're change makers, it can be earnest, let's be honest. We're passionate people, we're dealing with serious issues, we're making a difference in our workplaces, we're not running away from the world's pain, we're leaning into it. We can take ourselves overly seriously at times.

We also need freedom, fun, lightness, play, pleasure! We need joy – it's a massive energy booster! Remember your battery from Chapter 3? Joy makes you rechargeable! Joy is core to our humanity, it's a key part of how we stay sustainable. Joy forms part of our resistance to the dominant cultures and systems we're part of, a source of strength and hope that can sustain our momentum.

Prioritizing what you want and how you want to feel, and what can you do to feel that today, is not selfish, indulgent or flippant. It doesn't mean you're not engaging with the world around you, that you're not compassionate or sensitive to others. It's a valuing of your full humanity and allows you to stay refreshed and resilient.

What boosts your energy, gives you joy, peps up your motivation? *Find and relish those things!*

If you need inspiration, look back at your resilience map in Chapter 3. Or more ideas here…

Try going for a walk in nature, watching a documentary about a topic you know nothing about, reading a novel, leafing through a beautiful book of art, browsing the delicious recipes in a cookbook, baking brownies, growing veggies, make something crafty, drawing/painting/sculpting, playing music, dancing, singing, doing hair, painting nails, cuddling your kids, stroking your pets….

The options for pleasurable activities (that aren't about consumerism) are endless. What would you add? One of my favourite power practices, because it's so simple and has an immediate impact, is beauty spotting.

POWER PRACTICE   Beauty spotting

Take a walk. Urban or rural, near or far, it doesn't matter.
Find something of beauty, something that pleases you.
Take time with that thing, use your senses, enjoy expanding your sense of awe and wonder.
That's it!

STORY   Do more of what you love

When our kids were tiny, my partner and I used to take a day off work on our birthdays. We'd plan a long walk that we could do fast, and without little people asking 'are we there yet' and needing snacks every 50 metres. The best walks ended in a pub or café for a late lunch, before heading home. On one of these birthdays, we talked about how much we loved these days and the space together they created for us. I realized how topsy-turvy it was when we loved these days, yet we only had two of them per year! We could *do this more*.

Noticing the beliefs that were running for me that I could only give myself permission for such deep joy on my birthday, the constraints I'd had running in my mind ('it's tricky with child care', 'we don't have that much annual leave', 'we need to book ahead', etc) just fell away, and it suddenly became possible to *create more joy*.

We now have a walking day once a month. It feels like a treat, it feels special *and* it's also now a *normal part of our regular rhythms*. We book walking days ahead in our diaries and they're sacred spaces we look forward to, plan for and enjoy.

A monthly walking day with your partner may not be your thing at all. What's *your equivalent* of a walking day? What pleasure or moments of joy are you denying yourself? What can you start to put in place and make space for in *your* schedule?

Finding your joy in your workplace and workday is essential too. It adds massive value to your work when you're spending time on those things that you enjoy most.

You're likely to be playing to your strengths and finding flow (more in Chapter 5), which means you're likely to be doing your best work.

REFLECTION POINT

What do *you* most love to do?

What gives you joy – activities, people, situations, experiences…?

What else do you *feel* when you experience or do that thing?

When and how can you do that thing more?

Are there other ways you can feel more of how you want to feel?

....

....

....

....

....

Finding your yes

What are you saying 'yes' to? When you're clearer about what you want, saying yes (and saying no! – see Chapter 5) becomes easier.

Part of our culture of overwhelm and exhaustion is that we're expecting always to be in the season of Spring or Summer, always 'on' and always 'yes'. Part of our conditioning as women is the expectation that we'll be communal, people pleasers, prioritizing others' needs, with the default of 'yes'.

I've had to learn the concept of a discerning yes, that my yes is a choice. My yes needs to be 'enthusiasm' not just 'oh, ok then'. An 80–100 per cent yes, not a 20–40 per cent yes (consent is another whole connected topic here).

STORY   Discovering my 'yes'

I've flirted with burnout many times in my career because my 'yes' has been diffuse and generous! I've overcommitted and extended my efforts and capacity to hold more. One day I brought my overwhelm and sense of impending burnout to supervision. My supervisor told me I needed to refine my 'yes'. I was cross and her comment niggled me for days (usually a sign someone's said something we need to explore more deeply, right?!).

So, I explored it and started to see my 'yes' as having gradients of enthusiasm, that not all my 'yeses' were equal in terms of value and worth to me. Not all my yeses were 80–100 per cent enthusiasm. Some of my yeses were actually 60 per cent or even 40 per cent. I realized that refining my 'yes' meant I could actually start saying 'no' to everything that wasn't a high percentage of yes.

How can I discern my full-body 'yes'?

I'm talking through different client projects with a colleague. My mind's wandering and I check my battery energy. I notice I feel drab, depleted, no buzz as he's telling me about a new high-budget project, involving travel to Sweden, Italy, China and the United States. I'm curious about my reaction. I'm saying all the right things (I've learned how to match, build rapport and stay connected in a conversation!) but I'm not feeling it… until he mentions the gender and inclusion aspects of the work. I notice a spike of curiosity and burst of fizzy energy in my body. This part's a *yes*!

I'm learning that the 'yes' for me feels expansive, a bubble of air expanding inside me, my heart beating a burst of energy – as opposed to when something feels depleting, constricting, flat or low energy. It's work in progress for me to listen for my 'yes'. This essential practice gives us *golden* data.

My next wise supervisor taught me that as we bring more focus into our change-making work, we clarify our 'yes' even further. As we clarify and go deeper into our niche, it can open up again, and we need to clarify and distil even more. What used to be an 80 per cent yes is now just a 60 per cent or even a 40 per cent, and so what used to be a 'yes' becomes a 'no'.

EXERCISE   Full-body yes

How do you recognize your 'yes'? What are the body signs for you?

Next time somebody offers you an opportunity at work, or you've a choice to make – check in with your body. What do you notice?

- What feels constricting or contracting?
- What feels expansive?
- What are the signs of a 20% yes? 40%? 60%? 80%? Can you start to differentiate?

Start getting really comfortable with listening in and connecting with your body's 'yes'; it's another way of us tuning in to our inner wisdom. Check in with yourself at decision points throughout the day (just practise – cup of tea or cup of coffee?) – what's your body data? As you develop your muscle, check in with your body data when it comes to 'bigger' decisions, whether to go for new assignments and job opportunities. I ask any future collaborators, partners, colleagues, even clients, 'what do you love saying yes to?' It helps me know what makes them sing, what lights up their heart, so where I have opportunities I can offer them more of that.

I'm encouraging you to have a mix of work and change making, alongside other enriching aspects of your life that bring you joy. Your 'yes' is unlikely to be in just one direction!

Notice your jealousy

Jealousy can also give you a strong indicator of what you want. When we feel jealous of someone else's situation, circumstances, possessions, an achievement or milestone they've reached, an aspect of their character, or the way they behaved or dealt with a situation, our jealousy reveals more about *us* and the desires in our own hearts, than it does about *them*. Notice it!

We couldn't have this chapter about our desires and what we're saying 'yes' to without having a section on saying 'no' – it's coming in Chapter 5!

Having explored your joy and your yes, we're now going to build on your purpose and change-making focus.

What's your Ikigai?

Ikigai is a Japanese phrase that translates as something close to 'life purpose'.[6] It's a way of thinking about what you love, what you're good at, what the world needs and what you can get paid for. Often adapted into a career-planning tool, here I offer it to help you align your intentionality and what it is you want with your sense of change-making purpose and plans for the future (Figure 4.1).

Let's go deeper with your Ikigai

Are you ready for some research and detective work?

Work your way round each circle. Make connections with your thriving visualization from Chapter 3 and the 'what do I want?' reflection points earlier in this chapter.

FIGURE 4.1 Your Ikigai

As change makers you may already be connected into these aspects of your purpose. Use these reflection points as an opportunity to 'dial up' what you're saying 'yes' to, to refine your purpose and focus.

FINDING OUT WHAT I REALLY LOVE

Where do I experience most joy? Over the next week, start to track your joy levels and check in with your full-body 'yes' (see above). I had a big list of 'what do I love' and then when I checked in with my inner joy tracker, I realized there was a range! I refined it down to what I liked, what I loved and what I *really* loved.

FINDING OUT WHAT I'M REALLY GOOD AT

What are my strengths? Complete some tests such as a 'strength scope' questionnaire or 'leadership strengths finder', take an Enneagram personality test, do Myers-Briggs. You can pay for psychometrics like Insights or Hogan to give you deeper insights around your strengths. Explore your Zone of Excellence and Zone of Genius.[7]

Ask for feedback from trusted colleagues. You can say: 'Describe me in three words. What do you appreciate about working with me? What are my strengths?' You'll get lots of rich data!

Reflect on three recent accomplishments you're really proud of. What is it you did, what was your contribution? Write it all down.

What are the themes coming through this analysis?

FINDING OUT WHAT THE WORLD NEEDS

What are you most curious about in the world today?
What piques your interest?

Which section of a newspaper or magazine do you go to first? Where do you click?

When you watch the news, what breaks your heart?

What are you furious about, where do you rage?

What's an injustice that you want to see righted?

Imagine you're holding a magic wand that will make a difference... what do you do first?

Complete these sentences: I wish there was more... I wish there was less...

Sometimes we know the sector where we want to work, the area, the aspects of the contribution we want to make, and we need to research what the possibilities are for us specifically in that area.

What are the needs? Who else is working on it? What are others doing? Start to explore what you can add and contribute to what's already happening.

What questions do you have? What do you not know *yet*? What else do you need to find out?

You're looking for the match between what you love, what you're really good at, and the issue or area that you want to contribute to.

FINDING OUT WHAT CAN I BE PAID FOR

You may decide that your change-making contribution is going to be voluntary or pro bono, perhaps at least initially. Often that's how we build our experience, credentials and test out whether something's really for us. If you're looking for this piece of your life to also pay the bills, you need to explore whether the overlap of what you love, what you're great at and what the world needs can also pay you!

Build a research file of job adverts and job specifications. Look at the themes, the kinds of tranferrable skills that people are looking for.

Reach out to your network on LinkedIn or via email. Consider all the various roles needed in change-making work. What's the best fit for you and your mix of gifts and skills?

You're looking for the match between what you love, what you're good at, the issue or area that you want to contribute to and where you can get paid!

WHAT IF I DON'T KNOW?

It's absolutely ok if you don't know all the detail of this – yet! Keep researching, commit to listening in, keep your eyes, ears, heart open. In Chapter 5 we'll build on this; your detective work can be emergent.

REFLECTION POINT

Given all the analysis, research and data mapping above:

When you're living your dream life and making your dream difference, what's the contribution you're making?

Who are you helping?

What changes in your workplace because of you?

What changes in your community because of you?

What legacy do you want to leave?

What are you unconditionally committed to?

Ikigai, you can wake up each day and live with intentionality and focus, connecting to your values, centring your yes, your joy and finding meaning in the everyday.

2 **Discovering our purpose is emergent.** We rarely see the full journey at the beginning, it's as we start along the way that we start to see the path. You don't need to wait until it's crystal clear to start! We discover by doing, trying, experimenting.

3 **Your sense of purpose can emerge, shift and change through your life and career.** Precise details of the contribution you want to make may get clearer over time, or may emerge in different stages of your life, there's no rush. Consider your purpose story – you can find threads, themes, ideas that've tracked your life and left you clues.

4 **Purpose doesn't need to have an endpoint or a legacy.** Yes, I do believe we're each uniquely made and placed to find our space and bring our unique value, in the service of people and planet. *And* I don't believe it's a build and everything leads up to a pinnacle moment, with all the previous journey building up to 'this'.

5 **Our purpose is expressed in the small, small moments of life.** It's in the intentional living of our lives, in the present *now*, that we leave a legacy and build-up of who we are in the world.

6 **Your quest for purpose can't be at the expense of your mental health and wellbeing.** I've worked with a bunch of folks who're extremely 'purpose-driven', with a strong sense of bigger picture in their lives, who're also unhappy, burned out, exhausted in their day-to-day

existence. I don't believe your own desires need to be subservient or subverted to your sense of calling or purpose.

7 **Purpose helps us find our people.** When we move towards the area we're passionate about, that's where we find our people (more in Chapter 7).

8 **You're not too old and it's not too late.** Time is stretchy, remember! All we have is the ever-present 'now'. No need to disqualify yourself; there are abundant needs in the world and you have a unique contribution to make. Start tuning into your desires and seeking out then stepping into your change making. Start today!

Unwind rewind: chapter summary

This chapter is all about listening to yourself, knowing yourself better, trusting yourself more, discovering what you actually want for your life, how this helps you as a change maker, building out from your thriving visualization in Chapter 3.

We've explored tapping into your desires, your joy and full-body 'yes' in your work. I trust you're feeling confident that you can:

- get clear about the contribution you want to make;
- step out and experiment so your contribution gets clearer;
- have a way to listen to your core desires;
- connect with your joy and action your joy list;
- listen to your jealousy;
- be clear what it is you desire and what it is you want your change-making contribution to be, even as it's emergent;

- grow in how you're listening to yourself;
- increase your trust in yourself and develop your growth mindset.

So now we're clearer about what we want for our lives, our change-making work and contribution. How are we going to get there? In Chapter 5 we'll look at building out all the detail and we'll explore how bragging can support you in your progress (it's honestly better than it sounds!).

UNWIND REWIND

What's most important for you from this chapter?

What've you learned about your desires?

What beliefs do you have running for you about your desires, your joy, your 'yes', your jealousy?

In what ways can you see you've been conditioned around these aspects of your experience?

What have you learned about your purpose?

These are the things that give me joy:…

This is how I can do more of that today, this week and this month:…

YOUR CHANGE-MAKER PROGRESS + ACTION TRACKER

- My change-making contribution is…
- I do this by…. And in this way…
- I am saying 'yes' to…
- My start-point is…
- My best next step is…

- This is what I'll experiment with…
- This is what I'm noticing…
- Here's how I'll keep myself going…
- Here's how I'll stay accountable…

AFFIRMATIONS

'It's safe for me to connect with my desires.'

'I listen to my core desires.'

'It's safe for me to tell myself what I actually want for my life.'

'I trust myself.'

'I connect to my joy.'

'I'm clear what it is I desire and what it is I want my change-making contribution to be.'

'I'm growing in how I'm listening to myself.'

'I'm increasing my trust in myself and developing my growth mindset.'

'I feel fully alive.'

CHANGE MAKER INTERVIEW   Naomi Evans

Naomi Evans *is a teacher, writer, speaker and co-founder of the organization Everyday Racism which she runs with her sister, Natalie Evans. Her first book,* The Mixed Race Experience, *was published in February 2022. She lives with her two sons and partner.*

I talked with Naomi about her change making, how she stays resilient and overcomes barriers.

I'm a change maker because I'm encouraging people to become more active in making a difference, thinking differently about race and how racism works.

I want to put some good out into the world. Everyday Racism came from trauma. A bad situation which forced to me to reflect on how these things had impacted me my whole life. Realizing that I didn't want this chain of events to continue, I thought about what I could do to try and make a difference.

Growing up in an area where I felt very 'othered' has taught me what it feels like to be an outsider or not included. I think that's taught me empathy. I hate it when other people feel left out, and that's something that drives my work. Obviously, you can't please people all the time but you can try and do things, being mindful of other people's position and the way it may translate to them. That's why I think we need to get better at listening to those who have a different life experience to us, or we cannot cultivate empathy.

If you're looking to find your change-making contribution, take time to consider what makes you angry or frustrated. Often, it's those things that can lead you to where you can make a change. I often think about what I would like people to say about me after I'm not here. I think about what legacy I can leave in this world and work towards that.

On resilience

For me, resilience is about learning to accept that things will be difficult at times but it doesn't mean you won't bounce back. It's understanding that whatever you face will eventually pass and remembering all the times you faced other difficult things and got through them. It's also about knowing that one moment does not define you.

I know my triggers. When something affects me mentally or physically I am able to say 'I need to stop'. I am less worried about cancelling things or communicating that I can't do something. This means I am able to look after myself better. I'm aware of what helps me to feel better in myself, whether that's food, a walk, talking to someone. I used to just try and power on but I know for me that's not healthy.

On navigating barriers/bias

There are definite gatekeepers. In my work there are a lot of white men in positions of authority. They are promoted quicker and where women have time off to have children and then return part-time, their careers are impacted. This means a lot of men hold senior posts.

I've never been very forthcoming about advocating for myself at work. It's something I definitely want to improve on. I think there's a tendency to see people who speak up for themselves as 'trouble makers'. I think the system is set up against working parents and it's been a very stressful juggle trying to navigate that.

On the future of work

I think we need much more flexible working. Covid showed us it can be done. I believe we should all go to a four-day working week and people should have more holiday time. Working people into the ground is not a productive way to live.

CHAPTER FIVE

Change-making focus

'How will you get there?'

Decide what you really want to create in your life and say 'no' to everything that isn't that! ANON

You've met your future self, you're setting your intentions every day, and you're connecting with what you really want for your life. You've mapped out your Ikigai and considered your change-making contribution and legacy. So now you've done that big-picture work, we'll move into building out the detail in this chapter. How are you going to get there? How will you stay on track? And how will you know?

In this chapter we'll explore:

- Your brags and why they're so important!
- Mapping out your big-picture goals and breaking them down into small steps and WHTBD (what has to be done)
- Making it happen
  - Planning your moves
  - Keeping on track without burning out
- Getting it done
  - Finding flow
  - Shifting through procrastination
  - The brilliance of batching
- Setting boundaries, how your 'yes' shapes your 'no'
- Asking for help

Your brags

As part of my business mastermind, I often ask the group to 'check in' with their **brag** – something they're proud of from the previous week. It needs to be something they've done or progressed themselves (not their team). It can be very small, in fact the smaller the better.

The prompt is intentionally provocative and a deliberate unlearning. As women we're conditioned to 'not get too big for our boots'; we learn not to be the 'tall poppy' for fear of rejection and exclusion. Women tend to locate their success in external factors, whereas men tend to locate their success in internal factors.[1] This focus on a brag counteracts our conditioning that tells us we're valuable when we suppress our own desires, stay small and focus on pleasing others.[2] When we brag, we model for others and give permission for others to be open to new possibilities, step up and stretch into their change-making contribution too.

POWER PRACTICE   My brags

What was my contribution today?

What did I progress?

What is my brag today?

What am I proud of?

Take a note, however small. Do this every day.

Our brags help us notice the progress we're making towards our goals. As we complete tasks that are important to us, and notice the completion of small things, we build our belief and momentum to keep going for the big things (big wins are an accumulation of small wins). Noticing small steps and progress helps us see what's possible for ourselves; we build our possibility thinking and our beliefs that our change-making dreams might be doable. Noticing the pieces of work that we've completed gives us a sense of achievement. Achievement and completion are key factors in what makes us happy as humans. As we build our sense of what's possible, our self-efficacy increases, building our inner confidence and boosting our wellbeing.[3] Noticing our progress and our small daily 'wins' is so important and powerful to build our resilience, persistence and impact over time.

We're counteracting negativity bias, building our resilience through healthy mental habits (see Chapter 1). These healthy habits support us in stepping up in our change-making leadership and models for others that it's possible for them too.

How will you get there?

Let's start with the outcome in mind.

You've tapped into your deeper desires, you've identified what's in your heart that you want to change and the contribution you really want to be making. You've done the research, identified what success looks like for you and how you will know when you get there. When you're ready you can progress to making it happen – we'll look at making it stick and making moves!

Making it stick

EXERCISE Making it stick

1 **Create a vision board.** This is a creative process that taps into the intuitive part of you. Find old magazines, catalogues or papers, put music on and take 30 minutes to leaf through the magazines, cutting out anything that jumps out to you – this can be images, colours, phrases. Take a short break, make a drink. Come back to what you've cut and then create a collage. You can ask yourself the question 'what does it look like, what does it feel like, when I'm living my dream life, making my dream

---

difference' as you create your collage. Enjoy the process! Pin it up so you can see it.

2 **Write it out like a story.** Describe what's happening when you're living your best life, making your dream difference. Use 'I' and the present tense. Use these prompts:

a. I'm living in…

b. I'm working with…

c. My change-making contribution is…

d. The impact I'm having is…

e. It feels…

3 **Create a post-it version**. Write your story in three lines on a post-it. Stick it somewhere you can see it every day.

4 **Record your voice telling your story.** Send yourself a voice note. Read out your story. Use 'I' as in #2 above. Or speak to yourself as 'you', as if you're speaking to your best friend. Add in lots of affirmations (see list at the end of each chapter).

5 **Choose a body posture to embody** what it feels like to live as your best future self. Think back to your thriving visualization. Can you arrange your body into this posture and use it to ground and centre yourself? Some of my clients use yoga poses (warrior or tree are particularly strong poses).

6 **Tell a friend, coach, mentor or business mastermind companion.** Speaking your dreams out loud to someone else has a way of making them stick. You can ask them just to listen and hear you (rather than comment or critique)!

All these activities prime your brain for success.

Breaking it down

You know where you want to go. The direction of travel. The trajectory. This becomes your North Star, drawing you forward, helping you stay on track and keeping momentum. Now let's break the trajectory down into specific goals, then into tangible next steps or mini projects. Here's how I do it.

I get my vision board out, my mini story on my post-it, on a table in front of me, with a large piece of paper (I use decorator's lining paper). I've a bunch of felt pens and stacks of coloured post-its. I break down each area of my vision board into specific goals.

I then map out what has to be done (WHTBD) to make each of these goals happen. I get one task or idea down on one post-it. I then cluster the post-its. For example, on my vision board I'm earning a particular income and I'm making a difference through EDI consulting work, my business mastermind and my one-to-one coaching work with female leaders.

I break down WHTBD for each of these areas to be successful. One area I identify is visibility. So I read Chapter 7 of this book and then mind-map all the ways I can work on my visibility. Another area from my best future self visualization is writing my book. So, I break down WHTBD with regard to progressing this goal. I keep on breaking down each section until there are specific detailed actions.

What I usually find here is that there are more big goals and actions than I can possibly complete all at once! As

I shared in Chapter 2, my preferred season is Spring – I love this stage of mapping out new ideas and possibilities. When this generative and expansive strength is in over-play (a serious de-railer for me and potential contributor to burnout), it can lead to too many things on my plate. I need to bring in the Autumn energy of refining and select-ing, and listen in to my inner wisdom to get clear on what is my full-body 'yes' and what is a 'no' or a 'not yet/wait'.

I refine down the projects and give them a timescale. What projects have my full-body yes? Which are 60, 40 or 20 per cent?

Then I look at capacity, and start to cluster the projects into a timeline. What will be my focus in Q1, then Q2, Q3, Q4? What moves out into next year? What stays in the 'ideas' bucket for now? I work with my tendency to over-commit and overpack, and try (!) to build in lots of slip-page time, as well as space, in my year.

You know the rhythms of your year and your work life and specific industry. For me, January is slower, February to July is busy, August is a month off, September to November busy, then December is quieter. I consider my energy flows and the seasons for the year ahead and build in my Winter times of rest, quiet space, holiday. A gentle reminder: we're being counter-cultural here, thinking in seasons and cycles rather than taking the well-worn linear 'push through' approach.

Stepping back

Use the following reflection point to go deeper with your plan.

REFLECTION POINT

What am I most excited about as I look at this plan and
map of ideas?

Is there enough *joy* in this plan?

How can I stretch myself in my change making, how can
I take bolder risks?

Where is my full-body *yes*?

Does this plan prioritize and honour my wellbeing and my
resilience?

What are the best next steps?

Whom do I need a conversation with?

....

....

....

....

....

What to do when we're overwhelmed with options

Pick one area to begin. Start small. We learn more from
starting, doing, experimenting and tweaking (even if we
might need to pause and start again somewhere else later)
than we do from over-thinking and starting nowhere.

What to do when we don't know what to do

As we break down our goals and dreams into projects,
mini pieces of work, and as we break down each of these
projects into all the WHTBD and break it down again into

smaller pieces, we don't always know the detailed answers, so what do we do when we don't know?

We can go into **research** mode.

Make a list of the questions you have or the topics you want to know more about. Sometimes we know the sector, the type of work, the type of people. We know the general direction we're headed. These are clues that lead you to the next step.

Then use the three Rs:

Resources – find out the answers, use an internet search engine.

Remember – your own learning, what can you draw from your previous experience(s)?

Role models – who's done it before you, who's done something similar – pay them, learn from them, go quicker, faster, make fewer mistakes (you'll probably still make your own!).

STORY Making your vision a reality

My vision board had the goal of writing a book, so I then broke that down into the specific tasks and actions I needed to take. Writing the proposal, creating the outline, researching an agent, seeking a publisher, actually writing the book…. The launch and promo has another detailed breakdown plan.

For context, writing a book has been in my heart for many years, on my vision board for three, and started materializing two years after that. The methodical work to get it done and out into the world is two years. I share this with you as an encouragement and reality check of what it takes, that you

---

can do it too! You can place a dream out into the world and then work towards your goals.

So these big dreams take time but not in a 'I'll leave it' kind of way, but years of mulling and shaping the idea, then taking action. When we take the dream or goal out of our heart and head and put it out there, when we give it some focus and attention via our intention-setting power practice, we're priming our brains. Because you've primed your brain and heart, you'll see the opportunities that come up, you'll be focused enough to take the consistent specific action, you'll have in mind the goal which helps you achieve it.

There were lots of parts of this process that were new to me and I didn't know how to do it. I needed to research and explore to find out, so that I could then take action.

I joined a book proposal challenge to help me learn how and then actually do that part, I asked friends and colleagues in my network who'd also published books for their tips and insights, I reached out to contacts in the publishing industry for technical advice. I used the internet to research the publishing process and read books about the various ways to get a book into the world.

I also needed to allocate the time and space required for the project.

AT THIS POINT OUR INNER CRITIC WILL SQUEAK!

Our inner critic can freak out when we start taking action towards our goals! When we start to stretch ourselves and step up, it's the edge of our comfort zone!

Notice if some of this comes up for you:

- What if I fail…?
- What if others judge me (and imagining all the ways this can happen)…?

- But there's no point in me doing this, it's been done before, and others do it better...
- Who am I to do this? I'm just...
- Your own version of the above!

Remember your inner critic is wanting to keep you safe and it helps you do that by keeping you small. Tune into what your inner dialogue is saying to you (use the power practices in Chapter 2) and take a huge dollop of self-compassion to do the work to deal with it, so you're not sabotaging yourself at this point.

It's easier not to start

When creative ideas, new projects, things I want to start, change-making work that will stretch me, *stay in my head* they stay as a possibility. When these things stay in my mind it's less risky, it's much safer.

It's a form of procrastination. It's the notion that anyone can be an artist, but not everyone is willing to put the work in.

The fantasy version of this new project is better in your head than the reality. As you start to take steps to make that fantasy a reality, you realize how hard some of it is, you realize what you don't know, you see more of the effort you'll need to put in to make it happen. The end results are rarely what we imagine in our head. Keeping the idea in our head is infinitely easier than bringing it to life!

But progressing the *reality* of something, however less shiny it seems than it is in your head, is way more likely to take you towards your goals in life, than sticking with the fantasy and doing nothing!

Making it happen without burning out – here's the antidote!

As we explored in Chapter 3, the dominant culture (at least in Western societies) glamorizes the pressure around over-productivity, busyness, overwhelm, rushing and exhaustion. The masculine default model of 'always on' is generating burnout and mental health struggles, as well as increasing inequality gaps.[4]

In this book we're looking at an alternative perspective around intentional, cyclical and seasonal living. When we live in this way, prioritizing and valuing play, rest and joy, it's a form of resistance to our dominant culture, as well as valuing our full humanity. When we take the long view of our lives, that there *is* time, that we are not too old and it is not too late, we hold an antidote to overwhelm.

It's counter-cultural though, so it's risky to do. There are workplace demands and expectations from others. What are the conversations you can start having? Can you find your own 'system safety' so that you're able to speak to this from a place of groundedness? If you lead a team, if you lead a business, if you're an employee, who else can you find and speak to, and join forces with on this? How can you raise this issue with your employer? Chapters 7 and 8 have more for you on how to influence your organizational culture.

So now you have your big picture and your detailed breakdown. We're going to build out review and tracking cycles to help you keep on track in a sustainable way. This is not about 'hustle' culture and grind. We're not doing toxic productivity, remember?! This is about working to your rhythms, utilizing easeful ways to progress your goals and finding joy in the process.

Keeping on track

Do you ever get to the end of a week and wonder what you've done? You've definitely been busy, but not sure what you've progressed?

Maybe you're in a job that doesn't hold a lot of meaning for you, so shifting into change-making work or making progress towards it can feel like a big shift. It can be hard to squeeze that in alongside day-to-day pressures. Even if your dream contribution and the work you spend your time on day to day feel miles apart, even if you're working a full-time job and hold caring responsibilities, and there's not a lot of space for extra anything, I encourage you that you can be progressing, even in very small ways, to move your life towards your dreams.

Taking small steps of action every day, and allocating small windows of uninterrupted focused time towards progressing your goals each week, adds up to a lot of progress over time!

If you're prone to getting distracted or lured away from your own target by what others are doing, this is going to help...

We'll look at **daily rhythms** for staying on track with your dream, then build this out weekly, monthly, quarterly, annually.

This is about linking up your daily actions to your bigger-picture goals and dreams, so that the things you're spending your life blood, sweat and tears on day to day *are the things that actually matter to you.* Go back to your energy tracker from Chapter 3 and what you noticed about your energy, so that you can play to your strengths.

Building a daily rhythm

Creating a simple morning routine including intention setting (from Chapter 3) is a powerful habit to integrate into your day-to-day rhythms, even if you're someone who doesn't like routine and prefers to 'feel into' your day. You're starting your day with *you*, before anyone else's dramas, agendas or expectations come onto your radar. Go back to your thriving visualization from Chapter 3 to remind yourself what you're heading for. Visualize your best future self and start living as her today.

At the end of the day, focus on your progress, your contribution, your joy. Use the end-of-day power practice from Chapter 1. If you find yourself ruminating about anything from the day, use the golden questions from the shift out of rumination power practice in Chapter 2. Close the day with your gratitude power practice from Chapter 1.

Gratitude is a powerful way to counteract your brain's negativity bias, reset your central nervous system, extend your growth mindset and boost your overall wellbeing. I use the gratitude power practice every day as part of my morning routine; in the evenings, if I notice I'm feeling drained in any way by the day and to close my day positively; anytime through the day that I notice I'm in a fug and want to increase my mental clarity; shifting between activities or meetings and want to reset and increase my focus and presence; anytime I'm in a funk, my inner critic is dialled up or I notice I'm in fixed mindset or rumination mode in my thinking. You can use the gratitude power practice whenever you want to shift your state.

NB: clearly I'm a big fan of positivity *but* gratitude is not fake positivity, or toxic positivity, pretending that nothing that's happening is challenging or bad. We can be sold this idea of constant motivation and productivity, and anything less than that is us not living to our full potential. It's not human or realistic to be this way. It's normal and ok to not feel happy and motivated all the time. Gratitude is a robust practice, grounded in our lived experience, that helps us access authentic positivity in a natural way.

Building a weekly rhythm

At the end of the week, focus on your *progress*.

POWER PRACTICE   Weekly wins

At the end of your week, flick through your diary and schedule. List out everything that's happened for you this week. All the small steps. All the conversations you've had, the actions you've taken.

Note down any tricky situations you've tackled, a courageous action you've taken, the small ways you've stepped up.

Look back at the intentions you've set each day and the one thing you wanted to progress that's taking you towards your goals (from your intention-setting power practice). Notice what you've progressed.

Focus on what's shifting. Small things each week build up to big change over time.

I write these out each week, pencilled on to a small post-it – it's old-school! If you prefer an Excel spreadsheet or a mind map or whatever suits you best, go for it!

I take a moment to enjoy the memories from the week, to cheer myself on for the progress I'm making, to celebrate the small steps and the wins! I relish the feelings for a moment to 'lock' the benefits of that positive emotion in my brain and body.

I date the post-it note and put it into a plastic wallet. I've been doing this practice now for two years, so my wallet is chock-full of reminders of all the progress, small steps and learnings along my journey.

It's massively encouraging if I'm ever in a funk or needing a boost.

Building a monthly rhythm – what's most important to measure

What are your key measures of success? How do you know you're keeping on track?

There are so many things we could be tracking, and it can take a lot of time, so choose those few things that really are an indicator of the kind of progress you want to be making.

I review each month using the criteria of *impact*, *joy* and *money*, each a key value for me and a short-hand that I'm living my dream life and making my dream difference.

Impact speaks to my change-making work and desire to make a tangible difference in the world.

Joy speaks to my need to prioritize how I feel, to safeguard my health, relationships and wellbeing.

Money speaks to my desire to be building wealth, giving generously, while also paying the bills!

I use this trio to gauge what I'm saying 'yes' to, what I'm saying 'no' to, and realizing they need to be in balance, otherwise I burn out (no money, no joy, no impact!).

Use the following reflection point to consider your metrics.

REFLECTION POINT

What are the key metrics in your change-making work or in your business?

What's a simple monthly metric you can use to gauge whether you're on track towards your goals?

....

....

....

....

....

MONTHLY REVIEW

I hold a more reflective learning review with myself each month. Sometimes I take a walk, voice-note myself, write a post on social media or use my journal. I celebrate my learning, enjoy the feelings, make use of the insights.

Use any combination of the questions in Table 5.1. Allow what comes up. Use affirmations from the end of this chapter. Finish with your gratitude power practice.

TABLE 5.1 Monthly review

Key questions	Alternative questions	Affirmation
What's worked well this month?	What's lighting you up? Where are you finding your joy? What are you loving most? Where's the energy? What are you grateful for?	I attract joy I radiate joy I'm grateful
What's progressing?	How are you progressing towards your goals (track all the small things)? What do you want less of/ more of next month?	I'm making progress I seek progress over perfection I'm expansive I feel (name the emotion you want to feel more of)
What's worked less well?	What doesn't feel good? What's not gone as planned or as well as you'd have liked? What do you want to do differently? What are you learning?	I learn and I grow I embrace challenge I embrace change I flow
What qualities and characteristics were present last month and you want to celebrate?	How can you bring even more of that quality into your day/week/month ahead?	I am (name the quality or characteristic you want more of)

CELEBRATING PROGRESS BEFORE YOU MOVE ON

It's so tempting just to 'crack on', minimizing our progress as we move on to the next thing. Taking a moment to mark, notice, celebrate your learning, growth and progress is *key* to developing your change-making resilience. It feels like a small thing, but the impact is cumulative.

LOOKING FORWARD

Take a moment to look ahead (again, we're priming our brains for more of what we want). What do you want this next month to look and feel like, what do you want more of? What are you giving yourself permission for? Use the affirmations at the end of this chapter.

Building a quarterly rhythm

Your quarterly review is a brilliant opportunity to check in with your bigger goals, see how you're making progress, what results you're experiencing and any bigger shifts you want to make. I revisit my joy–money–impact metrics and I may also look at my Google analytics and SEO. You can reflect on the season that you're in and how you can embrace it, even with a small shift. You can explore what's the *gift* for you in this season. You can think about what you're learning, what you can do now that you couldn't do three or six months ago. The benefits of doing this are cumulative. It's brilliant to look back at previous monthly and quarterly reviews – this is where you really see the step changes of progress!

Join one of my quarterly Solstice or Equinox events via my site, where I run a guided reflection process to glean the lessons from the previous quarter and set intentions for the next one.

What to do with what you find out

It's great to track and review your progress... but what to do with what you find out!?

1 Notice
2 Celebrate
3 Tweak
4 Learn and grow
5 Keep going

Let's take each in turn:

1 **Notice.** Mark the progress. Notice what you notice. What's shifting, what's changing, what's consistent.
2 **Celebrate.** Celebrate the progress. Notice it (you're rewiring your brain, remember!). Is there also something practical you can do to celebrate? What would be a treat you can book in for yourself?
3 **Tweak.** Remember we're not ruminating, right?! We're going into *reflection mode* (see Chapter 2). What changes do you need to make based on your reflections and insights so far?
4 **Learn and grow.** Commit to the changes you want to make. Set your intention and plan the specific tasks.
5 **Keep going.** Consistent, persistent progress. Bursts and rest. Find flow. Think in cycles.

This is growth mindset and inner wisdom work *live* and in practice!

So you've got your plan, you're tracking your progress, now let's focus on getting your change-making work done! We're going to look at:

1 Finding flow
2 Batching
3 Procrastination
4 Setting boundaries
5 Energy leaks
6 Saying 'no'
7 Asking for help

1 Finding flow

Flow is that beautiful state where we're deeply absorbed and *in* our work. We don't notice time passing, we're 'in the zone', we're creative and generative, we're playing to our strengths. Flow states enable us to do our best work, our creative, intuitive, strategic thinking.[5] We can experience flow when we're alone working on a task, or when we're deep in a conversation with others. Flow not only feels really good, it enables us to be five times more productive![6]

CREATING CONDITIONS FOR FLOW

REFLECTION POINT

Can you start to schedule in time for *flow* each week?

This is unscheduled time away from other people's dramas, urgencies or agendas. This is a space to work on *your* goals, *your* priority work projects, *your* creative, strategic thinking.

> How will you do this? How will you carve out this time, and keep it uninterrupted?
>
> ....
> ....
> ....
> ....
> ....

What about finding flow *each day*? Sounds ambitious, right? It's likely not realistic to be in a constant state of flow, and if you've got a completely packed diary (like most leaders I know), you need to be super-intentional about creating conditions for flow.

Block flow time out in your diary. Safeguard that time. It's sacred. Allow others around you to learn to respect that boundary. Talk to your team and colleagues about why you're blocking out that time (they'll soon start seeing the benefits).

Connect to your rhythms (go back to your energy tracker from Chapter 3) and find out when's your best time of day to find flow. It may be more pragmatic than that – this is when my toddler's sleeping, or this is the only space I have that's unscheduled this week, so this is when I need to make this task happen!

Use batching. This power practice is designed to help you quickly and easily access a state of flow.

2 Batching

Research suggests we lose a significant percentage of effort, intention and focus every time we switch tasks.[7] Batching is a powerful technique to help us access flow, make progress fast and be more efficient with our time and brain power.

POWER PRACTICE   Batching

Pick a task where you'd like to make progress.

Carve out 30 minutes of uninterrupted time.

Close down everything else on your work station – no other tabs open!

Set a timer for 30 minutes.

Choose one aspect of your task to work on.

Focus on that task and go!

When your timer pings, you'll likely be in flow and not want to stop.

But take a break, stand up, get a drink, run up and down the stairs if you're able – take a moment of micro-resilience.

If you have another 30-minute slot, choose your task focus and go for another batch.

At the end of your day, notice how much flow you've accessed and how much you've progressed – now celebrate!

The research tells us we're more productive and energized at the end of a three-hour stint that we've 'batched' with small top-up micro-resilience breaks (remember these from Chapter 3?) than if we push through in one three-hour block.[8]

Batching has revolutionized how I work and enabled me to achieve big goals broken down and progressing, taking small steps over time. It's a habit and a muscle that we're developing. It might feel strange at first, but give it a go and experiment!

Use batching in two ways:

1 **To progress your change-making goals.** Link to your intention-setting exercise and decide what's one thing I'm going to progress today. That big task or goal can seem very overwhelming and it then becomes easy to procrastinate, but take a small piece of it every day. Batch your day into blocks and progress your change-making work!

2 **To progress all the itty-bitty things on your to-do list.** Batch similar tasks. For example, financial admin tasks like writing, sending, paying and chasing invoices; wealth-building tasks like checking your bank accounts, moving money into profits, savings, investments and giving pots; diary management tasks like scheduling meetings, booking travel and accommodation; people-based tasks like preparing for one-to-ones, personal development reviews or development conversations with your team. Do them in one go.

USING THE CONCEPT OF BATCHING THROUGHOUT YOUR DAY AND WEEK

Block out chunks of time and allocate these to particular focuses or tasks (use the following reflection point to assist you). For example, I've clients who keep Mondays or Fridays free for creative space, clients who block out Tuesday afternoons for team time, Wednesday mornings for business development calls, Friday mornings for team admin and so on. I've a monthly Friday blocked out for governance and finance catch-up. I've a monthly Monday blocked out for planning and big-picture strategy work. I've a monthly Thursday blocked out for content creation and PR work.

REFLECTION POINT

What tasks can I start to batch?

How can I use batching to help me create more flow in my week?

How can I create guarded 'flow time' each week and each month – even for some of each day?

What regular rhythms in my schedule can help?

....

....

....

....

....

---

3 Procrastination

Procrastination's likely to be present whenever we're stepping up and stretching ourselves to achieve change-making goals. Use your 'Recognizing your inner critic' power practice from Chapter 2 to notice your thoughts and feelings, and dig into why you may be procrastinating (Table 5.2).

4 Setting boundaries

Lacking healthy boundaries is a fast-track to burnout and exhaustion. Your 'no' is also expressed through the boundaries you hold. No-one else is going to hold your boundaries for you!

REFLECTION POINT

What boundaries do I want to hold this week?

What permission can I give to myself?

How can I prioritize my self-care, my own resilience, doing the things that give me joy, while also progressing towards my goals?

What conversation is needed and with whom?

....

....

....

....

....

TABLE 5.2   Procrastination

What do you notice?	Why are you procrastinating?	What to do	Power practice/ exercise to help
I don't want to fail	Fear	Explore what you're afraid of. What's the worst that can happen?	Recognizing your inner critic (Chapter 2)

(continued)

TABLE 5.2 (Continued)

What do you notice?	Why are you procrastinating?	What to do	Power practice/ exercise to help
It's too big, I don't know where to start, I don't have time to progress this big task	Overwhelm or confusion	Check you're clear on why you're doing this project Take it through the WHTBD breakdown exercise	Setting your intentions (one thing to progress today) (Chapter 3) Batching (Chapter 5)
I don't agree with this course of action	Not aligned	Take time to connect with your values and how you do want to proceed	Recognizing your inner critic (Chapter 2) What do you want? (Chapter 4)
I'm still figuring things out, it's not resolved in my brain yet	You're still processing	Take the mulling time! Enjoy the Autumn and Winter before Spring!	Activate your relaxation response *and* Breathing (Chapter 1) Top up your battery (Chapter 3)

STORY No one else is going to hold your boundaries for you

In my experience as a mum of two kids, working part-time, then full-time, then setting up my own business and growing it for over a decade, *no one else is going to hold your boundaries for you.* Your colleagues may respect them and work with them, but that doesn't stop people asking for things that will push you beyond your boundaries.[9]

At the same time, I didn't want my employers to make any assumptions about what my boundaries were. The data tells us that many women miss out on stretch assignments, promotions and extra visibility as employers make assumptions about what they will and won't want – particularly when part-time or parents.[10] I agreed with my boss that I'd rather hear about all available opportunities, and say `no, that won't be possible because of xyz boundary that I'm holding'. I didn't want them to assume that I didn't want to hear about opportunities or that I wouldn't be able to take them on due to family commitments. I wanted them to still tell me and ask me.

5 *Energy leaks*

I recently realized I was deleting several emails every day – marketing messages from a collection of random sellers of printer ink, plants, trainers I'd ordered during lockdown. This deleting spree accumulated into several minutes every day and created a distraction in my inbox, and although these were tiny tasks it was an unconscious 'yes' of my attention, access to my precious energy. Rather than deleting the emails today, I took the extra few seconds to unsubscribe instead. Asserting this 'no' felt really good, like plugging an energy leak.

Where are your energy leaks? How can you plug them?

6 Saying 'no'

You're not going to make the full contribution you want to make without focus and emphasis. When we're clear about our 'yes', it's a lot easier to say 'no' (see the 'full-body yes' power practice in Chapter 4).

When we're saying 'yes', we're automatically saying 'no' to something else (because we're not superwomen with unlimited capacity, remember!).

We can flip this too. When we're saying 'no', we're actually saying 'yes' to the things that we want. So, the 'no' is serving you and your dreams and the contribution you want to make. We're learning to respect our own time, when we say 'no, we have to do xx' (our change-making work, our focus on our joy, our wellbeing).

You're not just saying 'no' to that event or opportunity that's a priority for someone else, you're saying 'yes' to *your* change-making work. You're saying 'yes' to that early night and the sleep you need, *so that* you can do good work the next day.

You're saying 'yes' to building *your* dreams and *making the contribution you want to*. By saying no to that networking event, you're saying yes to the relationships you already have and want to nourish and enjoy.

> Stop trying to get an A+ at anything other than (doing your) best work.[11]

This reframe can help make our 'no' be a bit easier. It's also about the expectations we place on ourselves. Recognize your inner critic drivers here? We're not socialized for saying no, so our inner critic will squeak. It takes practice!

ELEGANT WAYS TO SAY NO

'Thank you so much for this opportunity… it's not for me. I can recommend…' (a brilliant opportunity to uplift someone else, see Chapter 7).

'I'm working on other priority projects at the moment.'

'Come back to me after….'

'I really appreciate you asking.'

'I appreciate you thinking of me.'

'I'm going to say no this time, please ask again…' (only if you'd like them to!).

Also, your boundaries and your 'no' can change! They're not set in stone and there's grace to shift and change as you transition through the stages of your life.

Back to my monthly review criteria of impact, joy and money. I use this gauge to hold my boundaries when I'm offered new things – client work, collaborations, speaker events and so on. There are nuances too, right?!

Something can be lower on money, but if it's high joy, high impact, I'll consider it. Something can be lower on joy, but if it's medium to high impact and high money, I'll consider it. Neither of these options can be my situation all the time – or either I won't earn enough to pay the bills, or I'll fill my time with work that saps my energy.

7 Asking for help – it takes a village!

Let's be honest with ourselves and others where we need and receive help. Women leaders saying 'I'm just really organized' when they're (so often) asked 'how do you do it, how do you juggle it all?', when actually they have a nanny, a cleaner, a housekeeper and so on, is unhelpful. For women looking on, this feels unobtainable, maintains the mystique of 'women can have it all', keeps alive the myth of the 'ideal worker' who can show up at all hours and be present uninterrupted for work. If the reality of our lives is less than insta-perfect we can feel like we're failing, when actually we're human. No-one asks senior men how they juggle it all, because the assumption is they're not doing it all, they've someone else in their lives who's handling the domestic, emotional and mental labour.[12]

We need to know the cost of what we aspire to, and we also need to be honest that it takes a village!

Let's be honest: when we've a hairdresser, a therapist, a cleaner, an admin assistant, we seek help and we benefit from it! We value these roles (which are often devalued and under-paid in our society) and it's an honest reflection of what it actually takes for us to be stepping up in our change-making leadership.

In every single area of my life I ask for help when I need it. This is my superpower. (Lauren Currie)

STORY   Holding boundaries, asking for help and how it takes a village

When we look at other women's lives (or even earlier stages of our own lives!), it's tempting to compare and despair.

My experience with parenting is that each stage shifts your capacity. I was only able to do what I could at each stage of my career because of where my kids were able to be at, and with the privilege of support from my partner.

I try to remember that different stages have different dramas and levels of pressure and strain. I didn't try to grow my business until the kids were quite a bit older. The pressure of starting your own thing with small kids is massive. My kids were both recently off and at home during the Covid-19 pandemic – my work days were a mess!

There's no need to compare; you're not too old and it's not too late. Everyone's dealing with stuff behind the scenes, most of which we don't know about, and it's kinder to ourselves not to judge. Go at your own pace, be present with the stage you're at and enjoy the journey.

Notice your inner dialogue here. What's this story bringing up for you? What judgements do you notice yourself making – about me as the woman telling you this story? About yourself in response to it?

Here's another opportunity to go gently, notice your inner critic and invite your inner wisdom to speak with you.

Unwind rewind: chapter summary

In Chapter 5 we've moved from the big picture of your change-making work into building out the detail. We've equipped you with ways to make your dream life, making your dream difference start to happen!

We've discussed what you'll track to keep momentum, finding flow, shifting through procrastination, the brilliance of batching and a way to use your 'brags' to support you in your progress. We've talked about setting boundaries, how your 'yes' shapes your 'no' and asking for help.

In Chapter 6 we're building on the inner and personal change-making work we've done so far, and going deeper into the outer and systems change-making work.

UNWIND REWIND

What's most important for you from this chapter?
How will you start to track your progress towards your goals?
What do you give yourself permission for...?

YOUR CHANGE-MAKER PROGRESS + ACTION TRACKER

- This is what I'm experimenting with (the action I'm taking to make a difference).
- This is what I'm noticing.
- Here's what I'm going to do with what I'm learning.
- Here's how I'll keep myself going.
- Here's how I'll stay accountable.

AFFIRMATIONS

'I focus on my goals and dreams.'

'I take inspired action.'

'I trust the timing of my life.'

'I have all that I need to support my goals and dreams.'

'I find willingness, help and support.'

'It's my time and I'm ready for the next step.'

'What I have today is enough to take me to the next step.'

'I celebrate my progress.'

'I release….'

'I let go of the old… I make space for the new.'

CHANGE MAKER INTERVIEW   Alice Olins

***Alice Olins** is founder of the Step Up Club, an advocate and supporter of women. With a background in journalism, she pivoted in 2016 and wrote a manual for women and their careers. The business now includes a thriving online membership, a 1-2-1 coaching business, corporate workshops and sell-out Step Up Club learning programs. Alice is the careers columnist at* Red *magazine and is about to relaunch her chart-topping 'The Success Revolution' podcast.*

I talked with Alice about her sense of purpose, her resilience, and how she values collaboration.

I'm a change maker because I won't accept the status quo for women, not just in the workplace, but in how they view themselves. I'm passionate about women fulfilling themselves, uncovering their passions, being able to articulate and communicate their needs, being respected whatever their career/life choices.

My purpose – my passion, my path – evolved over time as I realized I had a voice, I had knowledge, I had an ability to help women view themselves more positively.

I bring a personal touch, honesty, a truth that only comes with experiencing something extremely traumatic but ultimately allows you to speak with a resonance and authority that perhaps others can't reach, in the most modest way possible. This isn't a brag, it's just a truth.

On resilience

We all have more resilience than we give ourselves credit for, but that doesn't mean it isn't a stretch to 'find' it when the going is rough. Resilience is a process, not a personality trait, so we can learn ways to develop it within ourselves. The key, though, is to trust it in those harder times, because that's when it's easiest to deny ourselves our own strength. I've had to be hugely resilient in my life, and when you're broken and come back, you have more to give, more knowledge to share.

Managing my internal voice, and remembering and leaning on my support network, and finding time to rest have helped me enormously too.

On collaboration

The value is priceless! I have collaborators that keep my mind alive, help me think differently, allow me to take risks I wouldn't otherwise (sometimes there's a push involved) and generally feed everything within me that would wilt if I was alone with my thoughts.

I'm lucky that I've created a community that does all of the above, so professionally I'm supported and inspired every day through Step Up. Personally, I have spent a lot of energy and passion nurturing friendships and family relationships because people are my thing.

On navigating bias, barriers and opposition in the world of work

I've had instances where, as a woman, I was belittled and made to feel inferior. My voice is stronger with other women.

I face barriers and biases, both internally and externally, daily I'd say – we all do. Again, it's about transparency, feeling as comfortable as possible taking the risks required to counter it and having the conversations I need to have to understand what's happening and why.

CHANGE MAKER INTERVIEW Keiko Asano

Keiko Asano is Managing Director of Munters Japan, the first female MD for Munters. She's a mother and guest Professor for Diversity at Tokyo's Innovation University.

I talked with Keiko about how she stays resilient and navigates opposition in her change-making leadership.

I'm a change maker because women have such a high competence to contribute to society. My purpose is to help change women's mindset of what's possible. As company leader I believe making this change will make profit, earning not only money but also satisfaction for people. It breaks my heart when I see women who give up on improving.

On resilience

Resilience comes after a mistake and the awareness that comes. Once people can be over the incident, you go forward to the next 'wall'. Every human has this competence, in order to survive in life. The extent to which we can learn and grow is the extent of our profit!

On finding your change-making purpose

Find what you contribute as a point that is unique to you. I emphasize to other women that they're important to our business.

On role models

My role models are my friends. One is my Swedish friend who left the company but she always listens to my thinking and asks 'What do you think? Why do you think it? What would you like to be?' Another is a board member for a big Japanese company. She became a board member at the same time as I was made MD Japan of my company. I discuss things with her and learn from how she feels/plays/talks to people.

I'm supported by my friends, especially women. If I can improve more through this support, it's a big opportunity. My supporters in my network don't tell me what to do, they always ask me, so I'm always thinking to find the answers. This 'exercise rope' makes me step up!

On navigating barriers and bias in work

I'm still on the journey. My colleagues have not all realized that they (maybe myself) have barriers and bias. I'm finding what 'words' can open the door of their understanding. For a better gender balance, I created new manager positions to assign to women. Of course, everybody has the right to these positions but I push and prioritize women to apply.

On dealing with opposition to your change-making work

Happening all the time, everywhere! I try to show the reasons for the change, I try again from another angle, with other words. I explain the profitable areas to people, so they'll gradually follow the change.

CHAPTER SIX

Change-making barrier busting

'Who do you think you are?!'

For those who are used to privilege, equality can feel like oppression.

This chapter is all about how we navigate the systems that we find ourselves in, that we choose to join or to exit, and that we perpetuate. If we want to shift from where we are to where we want to be in our change making, an awareness of the systems we're in and their impact is essential. Otherwise we're ignoring the nuanced mix of enablers and blockers that most women and others with marginalized identities experience in the workplace, and when moving through the world. This leads to minimizing, denial and victim blaming, and negatively impacts our mental health.

We'll look at how bias creates an invisible layer that generates blockers and barriers, and at how you can build psychological safety and become a more equitable leader. We'll talk about microaggressions and privilege, headwinds and tailwinds, how we overcome bias, calling colleagues in and what to do when we're called out, 'not-all'ing, bystanderism and the difference between intention and impact.

This chapter is all about dialling up our systemic awareness, which, when situated alongside our dialled-up personal awareness from earlier chapters, is a dynamite combination for us as change makers and change-making leaders.

In Chapter 1 we looked at thinking errors and how our brains in threat response lead to bias. I suggested that to get good at creating more equitable workplaces, we need to get good at resetting our central nervous systems and accessing our growth mindset. Reading and working through the exercises in this chapter is going to be confronting, maybe even threat-response-inducing, so this is a great opportunity to practise!

Putting on the glasses to see barriers, bias and blockers

Bias plays out in all workplaces and in all human systems. Do you remember Jesse from Chapter 1, how we created a story and narrative about her, based on assumptions, prejudices and societal conditioning? It's how our brains work, we all do it, and it's how our society forms in-groups and out-groups.

These biases create systems of expectation about 'the way things are done around here', which are normalized as workplace and societal cultures. Bias is baked into every system. When it's unchecked, it creates barriers and exclusion, the presence of micro (and macro) aggressions, and undermines equity and inclusion.

This is a set of lenses through which to see the world. I invite you to put the glasses on – once you see, you can't unsee!

We can internalize our oppression, which is the idea that we start to believe and accept the misinformation, myths and stereotypes that society communicates about us as inevitable, and then we can turn the oppression on others from our group, rather than looking to dismantle the system itself.[1] For example, women do patriarchy's work when we judge and undermine other women.[2]

The intersectional aspects of our identity (from Chapter 2) also affect our lived experience and how it is for us to move around the world. Our experience of bias is contextual and also goes beyond individual experiences. Racism, sexism, ableism (and the other systems of oppression) play out intrapersonally, interpersonally, systemically and structurally across society.[3] I talked with Caroline Ellis, Director of Deeds and Words, about how she sees bias playing out inside organizations:

> My lived, volunteer and working experience of the LGBTQ+ movement from the 1980s onwards has informed and influenced my approach to achieving positive change, within

and across communities and organizations. The negative and stereotypical representation of individuals from any minority group or community breaks my heart, as those stereotypes become embedded in every institution and in all the systems we live and work in.

EXERCISE   Workplace bias checker: Part 1

Think about your workplace – who designed it?

Who was it designed for?

Whose needs does it serve?

Whose needs are prioritized?

Whose needs are ignored?

Here are some common beliefs and biases running inside workplaces and how they affect us

So many examples and experiences of bias came up in my change-maker interviews, and I've woven some into the discussion below.

AFFINITY BIAS

We're drawn towards people who're like us; it's the 'like and lazy' bias. Affinity can be built through common values, beliefs, hobbies, interests, experiences. Affinity bias enables us to build rapport, connections and make stuff happen! If unchecked, it also excludes and creates strong in-group and out-group cultures.

> As a young-looking female I've faced bias, especially early in my career, leading to me missing out on opportunities, having my abilities doubted, occasions where clients requested to see less experienced but older-looking male colleagues. I've been ignored in meetings, with discussions directed at my male co-founder, and come up against negative attitudes around my need to balance care-giving with working.

CONFORMITY BIAS

We scan for social markers of who holds power and we work to 'fit in', tending to want to conform to the leader and what they desire. Conformity bias enables organizations to function, for leaders to take and execute decisions, but it can also lead to 'groupthink', over-reliance on a leader and lack of safety to challenge. With a lack of sharing of team members' own perspectives and views, new ideas are less forthcoming and less refined through healthy discussion and challenge. This impacts originality and innovation which, over time, stifles organizational growth and performance. Conformity bias can lead to cultures of niceness (I recommend we're kind, but not nice!) and often has 'untouchables' (particular people who hold power and whose poor behaviour is tolerated and unchallenged).

> Difficult men in positions of power who think they're saving the world but are operating in the vortex of bad behaviour generated by the operations of their own blind spot.

> I work in a white corporate environment that's very hierarchical and dominated by middle-aged males. I've

learned what battles to fight and when. But sadly, when you're outnumbered by the system, sometimes it's safer to not say anything at all.

Gender bias is real in my work – male colleagues have different expectations put on them and the expectations on female colleagues are impossible to live up to. So many of my senior female colleagues are off sick just now – the only 'get out' in an institution that does not tolerate 'lack of competitiveness' in any way.

EVALUATION BIAS

Women and those who hold minority identities tend to be held to different or higher standards of work and judged more harshly.[4]

> You have to censor yourself a lot because of the risk of how people will receive you.

> Saying things that people don't want to hear, and them using the fact that I'm a woman/progressive to downplay what I say.

Ranee Long, an entrepreneur and business leader in China, shared her experience of bias:

> I've had a lot of barriers and bias playing out in my world of work; for example, I'm misunderstood that I'm not ambitious enough to make more money and achieve more in business. How have I navigated it? I tried to be who I am as a leader to myself and as an influencer to others by using my strengths of building people connections, collaboration, trust building, engagement, by being professional and by showing them a different perspective of success, which includes work–life balance and wellbeing.

DOUBLE BIND OR LIKEABILITY PENALTY

Women who display masculinized leadership traits such as assertiveness and directiveness are perceived as competent but are less well liked. If women don't speak up for themselves, they're not taken as seriously, but are more likely to be liked.[5] This likeability bias is layered for Black, brown and indigenous women with the trope of 'angry Black woman'.[6]

> I've experienced bias around being American and not behaving within stereotypical expectations for women, e.g. 'bossy', 'unapproachable' (due to being confident/polished/successful), 'aggressive'. Basically for exhibiting what for men are considered leadership traits! Talking it through with my partner helps, who is an Asian man and understands bias/discrimination and sees me as a super-powerful, capable leader.

It's a tricky balance to navigate. Absolutely be competent (Be brilliant! Be ambitious! Shine brightly!) *and also* dial up the likeability. That means extra warmth, smiles, being aware of the potential to bruise egos!

> I've tried to recognize it's an issue other people have, not a true reflection on me or my abilities, where I've been able to I've corrected misconceptions and I've always strived to meet the highest standards in order to prove myself.

THE ONLY ONE

This is a belief that there's not enough room at 'the top', a perception that there can be 'only one' (Black woman, gay person, disabled person…), and it's driven by a lack or scarcity mindset prevalent in our culture. If I believe I'm the only one who's 'allowed' to be here, this can lead to an over-inflated sense of competition and drive.[7] It's a divide-and-rule approach, fostering a sense of competition, believed to drive performance and accountability, but actually usually just rewarding those who 'fit in' to the dominant workplace cultural norm, serving to maintain the status quo of who's in power and what identities are rewarded. This bias also plays into the oft-touted critique of EDI that it's 'tokenism', and ultimately minimizes rather than opens up the talent pipeline and organizations' opportunities for everyone.

> The experience of being 'the only one' can also be a pressure to somehow represent that identity in the workplace. White males are allowed to be individuals, they're not expected to somehow represent whole groups of others.[8]

> Being a female in a male-dominated industry to being one of the few Black women too, as well as being a single mum. For me, it's about not hiding my differences but embracing them. If someone else doesn't like that, so be it.

MERITOCRACY

Meritocracy is the belief that there's no such thing as privilege, there's an equal playing field and success is about hard work. This belief denies the reality of inequities or systemic injustices.

EXERCISE   Workplace bias checker: Part 2

What biases do you recognize from these descriptions –
   in yourself? In your workplace?
What are the implications where these biases are running?

Which have you experienced in your work life? What was the
   impact?

This list of biases can be a challenging read! We find it easier to recognize bias and how it plays out *in others*, or in contexts around us. We find it harder to recognize bias in ourselves – which is in itself a bias called confirmation bias! Use the power practices we worked through in Chapters 1 and 2 to notice what thoughts and feelings are coming up for you in your inner dialogue.

Implications of bias playing out

Biases form an invisible layer that hinders and restricts, generates barriers, blockers and microaggressions, and workplaces where these are unchecked are holding people back and aren't safe, engaging places to work. Research shows that biases playing out negatively impacts on morale, belonging and engagement, retention, promotion, talent progression and pipeline, the balance and mix of who holds leadership roles, organizational innovation, risk taking and ultimately the performance of the organization.[9]

Research tells us that the most successful businesses (with metrics of highest operating profit, less risk, best innovation, etc) are those with highest levels of psychological safety and inclusion.[10] Psychological safety is a feeling of connection and belonging, that I'm not going to be penalized for being myself,[11] rather than having to 'bend myself out of shape' to fit in.[12]

Where workplace biases are running, it can feel very psychologically unsafe. For example, workplaces with strong affinity bias can feel very psychologically unsafe for those who don't fit into the dominant culture group or 'in-crowd'. In teams with strong conformity bias running, it can feel very psychologically unsafe to be different or raise any perspective outside of the dominant 'groupthink'. Women who are penalized for being 'too strong', 'too assertive' or 'too soft', Black women who are labelled as 'angry Black woman', will not feel freely able to bring themselves to work. Workplaces with microaggressions towards those who hold different identity points from those in majority culture create a toxic working culture for *everyone*.

> I've mastered the art of navigating the spaces I'm in. I quickly work out whether I'm 'safe' or not, who my support network is going to be and I learn pretty fast what's going to work, what won't and how I can protect myself. I try to be as open as possible but also hypervigilant and prepared for what might arise.

Put on your glasses – and keep them on!

Now that you've got the glasses on, you'll see the impacts of bias more and more! See what you start to notice.

EXERCISE   Workplace bias checker: Part 3

Have a look around your workplace.

> What's the gender balance? At different levels (e.g. entry level, graduate level, management level, senior managers, executive leadership team, board)?
>
> What's the ethnicity balance? At different levels?

> Are disabled people (with hidden and visible disabilities) able to access, then thrive and succeed at your workplace?
>
> Do people of all sexualities, genders and expressions feel comfortable to be themselves in your workplace?
>
> What is the gender pay gap in your organization? Ethnicity pay gap?
>
> Notice if you easily or immediately knew the answer to these questions, whether that data and knowledge is accessible and transparent to you, or not.
>
> What conversations could you have as a follow-up? What awareness can you help to raise? Is there a change you'd like to be part of?

Let's add another layer here and talk about microaggressions.

Microaggressions

Microaggressions are small, subtle behaviours directed to someone's points of difference, like age, ethnicity, race, sexuality or gender expression, disability. Microaggressions leak out our biases. They're deeply conditioned and embedded; as the microaggressor, you may not be aware of your microaggressions – they may seem inconsequential, or be in your blind spot.[13]

You can think about each microaggression like a small paper cut, seemingly insignificant, but imagine them happening multiple times a day, every day, and it's death by 1000 paper cuts. Research evidences considerable psychological harm to the individual[14] as well as impacting the psychological safety of your team, workplace retention and performance.[15]

> I experience microaggressions regularly. I've challenged it and nothing's really changed. I'll stay until it's too uncomfortable and then I'll move on. I'll be welcomed at my next workplace and then I'll likely experience that exclusion again. That's the pattern.

Workplace microaggressions include things such as asking 'how many years' experience do you have?' when belittling someone's contribution; asking 'where are you really from?'; confusing a person of a certain ethnicity with another person of the same ethnicity; repeatedly mispronouncing someone's name; ignoring requests to do something until a white male steps in; making jokes aimed at women or minority groups; raising your voice even though the person is able to hear you; making eye contact only with males in a group with all genders; interrupting someone mid-sentence; commenting on someone's well-spokenness; taking more questions from men than women; continuing to misgender someone.

> You often get ignored at events (especially when networking), as if you've nothing of value to contribute.

> You're often given quite menial tasks and given limited opportunities for development.

> Microaggressions were a huge reason I left corporate real estate. It's also not fun being the only Black person in a building of hundreds; even subconsciously, it puts you in

a space of being eternally grateful to be let in. Excuse my French but – f*ck that! Similar biases exist in tech but I at least realize I don't need to play small or be grateful, I can show up knowing that I'm an asset, not a token, I don't really have to code-switch and thus I can be my full self, which includes having candid conversations with the CEO.

EXERCISE   Workplace bias checker: Part 4

What microaggressions exist in your workplace? In your team?

When have you experienced microaggressions? Or seen them occur?

What role have you played?

When have you been a microaggressor yourself?

How do you respond to microaggressions? That happen to you? That you see around you?

Now that you know better, you can do better! How are you going to do better this week?

We'll discuss what to do about microaggressions below.

Let's talk about privilege

Privilege is unearned advantage, benefit, right, favour or special opportunity, experienced and accessed by people who fit into a specific group in power or majority, over other more marginalized groups.

Think back to your intersectionality map from Chapter 2 and use the reflection point below to consider your advantages or access, remembering this is nuanced, personal and contextual.

REFLECTION POINT

What privilege do you hold?

Which aspects of your identity afford you certain advantages or access?

Which aspects of your identity create a barrier or hindrance for you?

How has this impacted your life?

How do you feel about your privilege? Notice what comes up, no judgement.

....

....

....

....

....

Let's explore an analogy of **headwinds and tailwinds** to help us understand our privilege.[16]

Imagine with me for a moment. You're going for a run, if you're able, and you're running along the promenade in front of the sea. The wind is behind you, you have a tailwind. How does it feel? It feels like you're having a great run, right?

Then you turn around to run back the other way and now you're running *into* the wind. How does it feel now? How does this headwind change how you're running? And how you're experiencing the run? Is it less fun? Is it harder work?

When we're running with a tailwind, we tend to think we're having a great day running! Actually, we're just experiencing the extra boost, flow and burst of energy that a tailwind gives us. This can contribute to a belief that we're great runners and that we should be able to win races and enjoy running.

When we're running into a headwind we tend to experience the invisible resistance. Things feel harder, we get tired quicker. This may contribute to a belief that we're not actually good at running, that we're not going to win races, and leave us feeling less encouraged and excited. You can see the link here with the internalized oppression we talked about earlier in this chapter, and how our belief systems work from Chapter 1.

Headwinds are an invisible layer of bias showing up, creating resistance, barriers. Tailwinds are aspects of our identity that open doors and mean that we 'fit', with opportunities and ways others have helped us through mentoring, support, training, offering expertise, opening up access... there are myriad ways that tailwinds help us and support us in our lives and careers.

Just to clarify, whether we're running with a headwind or a tailwind has nothing to do with us – we didn't create or 'deserve' either.

Use the following reflection point to review your experience of headwinds and tailwinds.

REFLECTION POINT

What headwinds and barriers have you experienced?

What tailwinds and enablers have you experienced?

....

....

....

....

....

Most of us have a mix! We experience privilege and the bene-fits of tailwinds in some aspects of our identity and in some contexts, and headwinds in others. There are multiple nuances here. I've experienced headwinds due to my gender and, at times, my age. But also, as a white, able-bodied, cis-gendered, heterosexual, neurotypical woman, with educational and wealth privilege due to my background, I acknowledge considerable tailwinds in my life.

How headwinds and tailwinds help us understand our privilege

Our negativity bias (Chapter 1) means we tend to take disproportionate note of the barriers we face, compared with the benefits we enjoy. We also tend to believe that the challenges we experience are harder than those faced by others. This focus on our struggles makes it tougher for us to appreciate the opportunities we've received. We mini-mize the impact that advantages and good luck have had on our lives, while vividly recollecting our ordeals. With others it's flipped: we'll downplay or overlook the head-winds and may treat as suspect attempts to bring equity by considering the headwinds others face.

We tend to look at others who're running the race alongside us and not acknowledge the headwinds they may be experiencing. We tend to wonder to ourselves (or out loud!), why aren't they achieving like me? We're all running the same race! There must be something wrong with them! This reinforces the biases we already hold.

A belief in meritocracy suits those who hold privilege and power: it blames anyone who's not 'succeeding' for 'not working hard enough' and sidesteps any culpability or accountability for transforming the system. If we benefit from tailwinds and don't acknowledge headwinds, then *of course* we're going to be all for sustaining that system of power that we benefit from. It suits us not to acknowledge that headwinds and tailwinds exist! This is how we can spot where we uphold and perpetuate systems that benefit us, rather than choosing to disrupt or dismantle.

Privilege begets privilege. For example, access to a particular university college grants you access to a meeting with the university fellows, and that allows you to have a conversation with X person, who introduces you to Y person, who offers you an internship, where you meet person A, who mentors you, and connects you with your first job at Z agency. If you believe in meritocracy and there's no such thing as privilege, you'll think that your hard work has enabled your success. Of course, you may well work hard; it's just not the full picture. The impact of generational wealth is another way that privilege tends to beget privilege.[17]

There's also a gender difference here: men will tend to associate and credit their great running performance with their own excellence, i.e. intrinsic to them, not seeing that they're running with a tailwind. Women will tend to credit their great performance with external factors: I'm having a good hair day, it's my great team, or luck.[18]

Co-creating new systems that allow access and fairness to all, that enact and embody justice and equity, requires us to give up some privilege and power. If we hold privilege in a system, it's our job to dismantle the system[19] – it's on us to notice how bias plays out, interrupt and disrupt bias in our spheres of influence, call out microaggressions, call in others in positions of power. It's not on those who're oppressed by a system to do the work to call others in and educate them about their needs.

Notice how it feels to acknowledge our privilege – it can be super-discomforting and uncomfortable: some people describe it like a spiritual awakening. When I run this enquiry exercise with teams of leaders, the light bulbs are pinging on!

White privilege

White privilege can be a particularly threat-response-inducing concept! Because the system of white supremacy we live within upholds whiteness, if you're white, you've got a tailwind (and you're not experiencing the headwinds of systemic and structural racism). You may well have worked very hard to get to where you've got to. You may have struggled during your childhood, or much of your life. You may experience significant headwinds because of your disability, neuro-diversity, sexuality, age, socio-demographic background or other aspects of your unique intersectionality map. Holding white privilege doesn't mean you've had an easy life, or haven't worked hard. It simply means that you haven't been held back due to the colour of your skin.

Use the following reflection point to explore your privilege.

REFLECTION POINT

How do you perpetuate systems of oppression?

How are you complicit in patriarchy, whiteness, heteronormativity, ableism?

What can you do to educate yourself more about systems of oppression?

What you can you do to start dismantling and disrupting?

What will you do differently (remember Maya Angelou's encouragement that 'when you know better, do better')?

....

....

....

....

....

These are *big* questions.

Checking in

As well as alerting you to systems, how we are in them and how they are in us, and as well as sharing thoughts on how to navigate them, this book is about resilience, wellbeing and your sustainability as a change maker. My hope is that you can get comfortable engaging and getting discomfited and disquieted by this work, and remain able to be present, chipping away at your part of the wall! Your resilience and wellbeing are key.

How are you feeling as you work through this chapter? Take a break, stay hydrated, get snacks, breathe, reset your nervous system! Check in with your inner dialogue and what's coming up for you.

You may find yourself with various objections.

I'll address them here.

'What if I don't see bias?'

In every client system I've worked inside, someone will say to me, at some point, 'I don't see how bias plays out', 'I don't experience it' and 'it doesn't happen around here'.

What about you – is this discussion new to you?

This is part of your privilege if you've not seen these aspects of workplace and societal life playing out, live before your eyes, and impacting your day-to-day life. Just notice, no judgement!

Listen to others' stories (like the examples above). There'll be multiple stories (in whatever sector you work in) that reveal to you the nuances of how bias is playing out, who holds power and how do they use it, how people are experiencing microaggressions and whether you've created a psychologically safe workplace where performance, morale and engagement are high and people are thriving. Curiosity is your asset here – start listening, stay humble, see how much you can learn from others' lived experiences.

I invite you to look at the statistics below. I've selected a few which give headline data revealing a piece of the picture of barriers that exist, and the implications for leadership pipelines, who holds senior positions and who has access and power inside these systems. In each of these examples there'll be layers and layers of story beneath the statistics!

The percentage of women in FTSE 100 boards is 38 per cent and 35 per cent for FTSE 250 boards.[20]

In 2020, 8 per cent of FTSE 100 companies had a female CEO, compared with 3.6 per cent among FTSE 250 companies.[21]

There are more men called Dave than there are women running UK funds.[22]

Although overall the gender pay gap has fallen slightly, it will take 60 years to close the UK's current pay gap. The time it will take to close the global gender pay gap has increased from 99.5 years to 135.6 years.[23]

Ethnicity pay gap reporting is still to be made mandatory in the UK.[24]

FTSE 100 companies reported 3.2 per cent representation of people with disabilities among their employees, compared to 18 per cent in the wider population with a disability.[25] Thirty-five per cent of LGBTQ+ staff have hidden their identity at work for fear of discrimination. Ten per cent of Black, Asian and minority ethnic LGBTQ+ employees have been physically attacked by customers or colleagues in the last year. Nearly two in five bi people (38 per cent) aren't out to anyone at work.[26]

Seventy-six per cent of white employees consider themselves allies to women of colour, but only 39 per cent confront discrimination when they see it, and only 21 per cent advocate for new opportunities for women of colour.[27]

You can dig into the statistics on representation, pay and lived experiences for people whose identity falls outside the dominant culture in your particular work sector – there'll be data!

REFLECTION POINT

From just the few stories of bias and data points we've shared here:

What feels familiar for you, what have you experienced or come across yourself?

If these statistics don't feel 'close' for you personally, who do you know who may be impacted directly? An employee? A team member? A colleague? A family member? A neighbour?

Consider that these statistics reflect actual people and their lives.

Consider what talent is lost. What struggle and suffering are caused. What potential is wasted. What possibilities of innovation and creativity we could be accessing as businesses, companies and wider society.

What is the impact on our shared humanity?

What feelings come up for you as you reflect here?

Just notice, no judgement.

....
....
....
....
....

Let's keep going with your objections

'WE'RE DOING WELL, OUR REPRESENTATION IS GOOD, WE DON'T HAVE A PROBLEM'

It's great if your top-line data is improving and there's a perception of making progress. However, dig deeper into the data, into the intersectional nuances, and listen to the lived experiences of people who don't hold dominant culture identities. You need to go beyond the optics.

'IT'S NOT HAPPENING HERE... NOT ON MY WATCH!'

So many middle-aged white male senior leaders have said this to me when I've just shared data on the way bias plays and microaggressions are happening inside their business. It's normal and human to feel resistance and defensiveness. This is not about good or bad, we all have bias. It's humbling and confronting to hold up the mirror and realize yes, even me, even you. Take a breath. Know that it's very likely happening in your workplace, you're just not aware of it yet.

'BUT I'VE NOT PERSONALLY EXPERIENCED BIAS OR DISCRIMINATION... I'VE NEVER EXPERIENCED MICROAGGRESSIONS'

If you haven't experienced any of these biases or microaggressions that we discussed, it's a sign of your privilege. Notice that you may be in resistance, defensiveness or denial.

Yes, some women haven't experienced bias overtly – your identity has allowed you to fit into the dominant workplace cultures that you've been part of and, again, this is part of your privilege. Examine your underlying beliefs here. Do you believe that other women aren't as talented as you, or that others haven't worked as hard? There are headwinds and tailwinds at play.

As you read about microaggressions, notice that your inner dialogue may be saying 'it doesn't happen to me, therefore it can't be real or true'. It takes humility to realize that just because you don't experience something personally, it doesn't mean it doesn't exist for others. In this book I'm inviting you to engage with and develop your change-making leadership in areas that may not directly impact you. I'm inviting you to see the wider systems and structures in workplaces and society. I invite you to be open to hearing others' stories; it may be confronting and humbling, but it also deepens our compassion, humility and empathy when we realize the privilege we each hold.

'NOT ALL...'

When white people say 'not all white people' in response to a racist incident, it's like when men say 'not all men' in response to incidences of violence against women. It's a way of separating ourselves from 'those' 'bad' 'racist' or 'sexist' and 'misogynistic' people 'over there'. It's denial, a form of gaslighting, avoidance, and another way of minimizing others' lived experiences. We know that not all men commit violence against women, we know that not all white people commit racist violence.

Let's focus instead on the system.

The problem isn't men, it's patriarchy.
The problem isn't white people, it's white supremacy.
The problem isn't straight people, its homophobia.
Recognize the systems of oppression before letting individual defensiveness paralyse you from dismantling them. (Ruchika T Tulshyan)[28]

Cultures of violence against women start with allowing and tolerating seemingly 'harmless' banter, misogynistic language and microaggressions that escalate. Cultures of racist abuse start with allowing and tolerating seemingly 'harmless' jokes and racist language, which escalate to racial microaggressions and beyond. Again, we can assume the system is 'out there' (it's another way of relieving ourselves of any responsibility), but actually it's 'in here', it's the sea we're swimming in, the oxygen we breathe, the conditioning we've imbibed.

On one hand, it's not personal (no need to get defensive). On the other hand, it's deeply personal – you can do something about it! As we're saying throughout this book, you are powerful, and this is a place to get curious about your power and start to use it. I am in the system and the system is in me – I choose to unlearn my racism, sexism (ageism, ableism and so on) and relearn. I choose to place myself at the wall and chip away!

Gina Martin notices that rather than debating 'not all men', those men could be using that energy instead to stand up against violence and misogynistic culture.[29] Nova Reid encourages us to spend less time on 'not all-ing' and more time on taking action to dismantle racism.[30]

How do we make sense of this picture as change makers? What's possible?

Consciousness and intentionality are key. Joe Gerstandt says that 'if you do not intentionally deliberately and proactively include, you will unintentionally exclude'.[31] Catrice

M Jackson says 'we need an anti-racism plan, otherwise we plan to be racist'.[32]

I don't believe 'allyship' is a one-off thing nor 'ally' a role that you acquire. It's a verb, an ongoing process of doing. We don't choose to say we're allies (others may experience our allyship), we choose to *be* allies and *do* actions that express our solidarity with others. I'm inspired by Privilege to Progress co-founders who use the expression 'show up' to mean 'moving through life with humility and solidarity'. Showing up is not self-congratulatory or performative; it's a consistent process of learning and action, 'using the privilege you have for progress'.[33]

In this section, we'll look at the difference between intention and impact, what to do to overcome bias in ourselves, what to do when you act on your bias as a microaggressor, how to challenge others in their bias, and a privilege superpower audit.

The difference between intention and impact

This insight was mind-blowing and revolutionary once I really got my head around it.

It's unlikely that you mean to be, or want to be, racist, ageist, ableist, transphobic. You're probably not intentionally perpetrating microaggressions to be mean or bullying to others.

So, this is not about your *intention*. It's about the *impact* you can have.

Your intention may be to have a laugh and a joke at work, to create a fun atmosphere, but the impact when someone else is the butt of that joke is that this person feels hurt, others feel awkward and no-one's having fun.

When we see leaders, celebrities or those in the public eye being called out, we often then witness their responses of defensiveness and victim blaming, gaslighting and separating themselves from the situation. 'I'm sorry if you felt that, or if that hurt your feelings' isn't really an apology!

Again, intention versus impact – you may well not have intended to hurt someone, or may have behaved that way through ignorance rather than malice or spite; however, the impact is still harmful and damaging. Remember death by 1000 paper cuts.

What to do to overcome bias in yourself

1 **Get curious and educate yourself.** Learn about different biases and consider how and when they might show up for you in your change-making leadership. Be super-aware and conscious of these moments and trigger points so you can mitigate this bias in your decision making and day-to-day interactions.

2 **Notice that it's happening!** Take a moment to acknowledge and notice.

3 **Challenge yourself.** Say 'really?!' What else do you know, what other information counteracts this bias or what might be another way of looking at the situation? When you assume that your female colleague will want to go part-time after the birth of her baby (it happens all the time), can you stop yourself, check in and get curious about what assumptions are kicking in there? Would you ask the same thing of a male colleague about to become a parent?

4 **Seek out new stories.** Read novels from POC (people of colour), queer, disabled writers, seek out different voices

and political perspectives, working class, trans voices. Read history that centres the national indigenous experiences rather than the oppressor or colonizer perspective. They might initially 'jar' with what you are used to – that's the point! Through this we give our brains a wider pool of exposure and experiences. New neural pathways, new thinking habits, new assumptions form.

5 **Be accountable.** Find a buddy. Create some accountability for your behaviours.

It's all about expanding our awareness! Back to Caroline Ellis, who encourages us to have conversations where we 'connect as complex human beings' as these 'act as a counter-balance to damaging stereotypes'.

Calling out, calling in – what can I do when I'm a microaggressor?

When we run workshops on inclusive leadership and creating psychologically safe workspaces, the number one thing that comes up is 'how do I call out challenging behaviours?', 'how do I challenge my peers?'.

I invite you to first recognize your own microaggressions! We move between positions of denial, passive acceptance, collusion and bystanderism (Figure 6.1) and then into deeper awareness, analysis and action.

When you recognize yourself as a microaggressor, feel the feelings, offer yourself forgiveness, don't hold on to shame or guilt. Offer yourself grace to learn and do better; remember your growth mindset (Chapter 2). Recognize the difference between your intention and the impact. Say sorry, correct yourself. If you've caused harm, then notice that, acknowledge it and apologize to the person. Don't

FIGURE 6.1 You and microaggressions

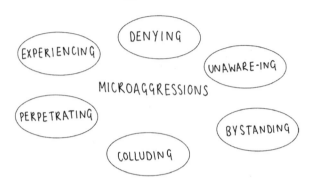

make it all about you, don't centre yourself and your uncomfortable feelings. Move on, stay curious, stay open, keep educating yourself.

If you're in this work and genuinely wanting to learn and grow as an equitable leader and change maker, you *will* get called out. Actively cultivate relationships with colleagues where there's enough trust and psychological safety that they'll call you in. How you respond to feedback is a critical predictor as to how much you'll get, how useful it'll be and how much you will or won't learn and grow as a change maker, leader and ultimately as a human. Start building and investing in these relationships now. Keep developing your growth mindset and system-soothing muscles!

As you want to start calling others in, it can feel tricky in the moment; we don't want to expose ourselves to ridicule or become the butt of the joke ourselves. We're sensitive to power dynamics and we want to fit in.

Find a way that feels safe to you – telling your manager privately, taking someone aside for a one-to-one. It's not an easy conversation to have *and* you'll feel better that you did it than if you didn't. Like a muscle getting stronger over time, these kinds of conversations also get easier with time and practice, so keep practising!

The UHT framework in the box below can help you to prepare for your conversation, stick to the message, not get side-tracked and not take it personally. As with any feedback, focus on the behaviour, not the person. You're sharing what you noticed in someone else's behaviour and the impact, not judging that person's intention, values, morals, lifestyle and so on.

EXAMPLE   Tackling microaggressions using UHT

UHT stands for:

Understand

However

Therefore

I **u**nderstand that you… (state intention)

However… (state impact)

Therefore… (state what you'd like to see change or be different, what needs to stop or start).

Here's an example:

*I **U**nderstand that you made that comment as a joke and you want to create a fun atmosphere of banter within this team. **H**owever, the joke is exclusive to those few who understand it, it excludes others who don't and it pokes fun. It's a microaggression. **T**herefore, I'd like you to stop*

---

sharing those kinds of jokes. Let's find other ways to make this team a fun place to be. If we need to learn more about microaggressions and creating a psychologically safe workplace together, let's do that.

WHAT DO I DO WHEN I'M CALLED OUT?

1 **Breathe** – you'll be going into threat response (see Chapter 1). Ground yourself and calm your central nervous system (use the breathing power practice from Chapter 1). This may feel *very* uncomfortable right now, but you're not actually going to die.

   So often (as white people) we stop here, and don't go deeper, because the feelings of discomfort seem so overwhelming and difficult. This is why it can come across that we care more for our own comfort than the protection of Black and brown bodies.

2 **Notice** the flood of feelings. Notice the fight or flight response in your body's reaction. Choose curiosity.

3 **Listen.** Take in the words, take in the feedback.

4 **Breathe.** Keep breathing….

5 **Play back what you've heard.** This demonstrates that you're listening, gives you a moment to process what you're hearing. 'I've understood you to say… this happened… and you feel… have I understood that correctly? Is there anything else you want to let me know?'

6 **Take a moment to process.** You may want to take a pause at this point. 'Thank you so much for sharing this with me. I'm going to process what you've shared with me and I'll get back to you. Let's talk again on…'

7 **Notice how you feel, notice the fragility.** The flood of defensiveness. You may also feel fear, guilt, shame, disappointment, anger, rage. This is normal and it's also part of how white-supremacy culture has shaped us and conditioned us.[34] Notice it, sit with it, use the power practices in Chapter 2.

8 **Apologize.** Actually say the words 'I'm sorry' 'I apologize'. As a full sentence. There's no 'but'. There's no need to explain, nor justify, nor defend. You may need to practise this, if the 'no buts' concept is new for you!

9 **Receive a correction**, if that's needed. 'What would you like me to do differently?' 'What would you like to happen now?'

10 **Move on.** Don't make it about you. People who are experiencing racial microaggressions don't need your white guilt and fragility alongside the impact of the microaggression itself. Take your feelings and your learning to your supervisor, line manager or coach. Journal, use the prompts from our shifting out of rumination power practice from Chapter 2 to help you process the experience, developing your growth mindset.

11 **Reflect on what you learned.** Do you need to go deeper? Do you need to educate yourself? The answer here is most likely, 'yes'! This is how we stretch and grow. This is how you dig into your growth mindset. How will you do that? There are fantastic educators who share free resources and paid programmes you can join.

12 **Do better next time!** When we know better, we do better. Shame is not a productive feeling to get stuck in. Let's keep it moving.

13 **Decide to disrupt the system and take action daily.** More in Chapter 8.

EXAMPLE APOLOGIES

'I'm so sorry I mispronounced your name. Thanks for alerting me to that. How do I pronounce your name correctly?'

'I'm sorry that I touched your hair. I realize that was harmful.'

What can we do about our privilege?

It takes humility to acknowledge our own privilege. It takes courage to work through the discomfort, and compassion for ourselves to choose a growth mindset around our learning. It takes intentionality and focus to not just 'park' this work, but to actually 'do the work'.

I've noticed that it actually becomes a tender joy to hear others' stories. It's fascinating, it opens up my thinking. I notice now how expansive I find the experience. I notice how my compassion and empathy increase as I connect with others' lived experiences. I notice how my commitment and determination to do what I can to make a difference increases. The purpose of anti-racism work and educating ourselves about equity and inclusion is not personal development, *and* I do believe that enabling us to become better humans is a by-product.

As women we've usually experienced a mix of headwinds and tailwinds and we may be navigating a strange tension of being both 'the oppressed' and 'the oppressor'. At times we experience headwinds, while at the same time we're benefiting from tailwinds that others don't benefit from.

I understand people's scepticism about white women and white feminism. There's a long history of white feminism ignoring or even progressing off the backs of Black, brown, and indigenous women. There are patterns of white women prioritizing their own comfort over justice for others.[35] White women already hold significant privilege and power, so if they (we) aren't taking an intersectional approach and disrupting systems, we're centering more advantage rather than liberation for all.

When we can acknowledge our own identity and the privilege we carry (use Chapter 2's intersectionality map); when we can hold our own identity without guilt, blame or shame; when we recognize that I am in the system and the system is in me; when we see that we can choose to 'decolonize' ourselves, that we can unlearn and relearn; when we know in our depths that this is a lifelong journey, a central piece of our change making, a work in progress; when we accept that we're going for progress not perfection... we can activate ourselves and start anyway!

This opens up my privilege as a superpower![36]

Superpower audit

Get curious and consider your privilege superpowers inside your workplace, and your wider life:

1 **Space at the table** – invite others into the rooms where you have access (panels, speaker gigs, board meetings, presentations to senior team, etc).

2 **Opportunity** – open doors for stretch assignments, promotions, exciting new projects. (Who do you usually offer these to? Do they look and sound like you?!)

3 **Visibility** – who can you speak about or mention, whose work can you affirm (so many women tell me how senior colleagues consistently take credit for their work)

4 **Decision making** – for stretch assignments, mentorships, training and development, career progression, promotions, lists of 'talent', opportunities for growth – advocate for those who have less privilege and access, and who may not be in the room when these conversations are happening.

5 **Alongside** – amplify your colleagues' voices and ideas (we know women and marginalized groups routinely have their ideas snatched, take up less air time in meetings and yet are spoken over and interrupted at a higher rate than those who fit majority workplace culture).

6 **Sponsorship** – you might be mentoring others and acting as a sponsor for others' development already – that's great. Just take a scan and check: do they look like you? Do they look like the norm and default in your company?

7 **Supply chain** – where and from whom do you buy, sell and contract work? How can you extend business to a wider group of connections? What systems of privilege and access can you start to disrupt and dismantle? Think about the whole 'supply chain' of your life: who do you buy from (you can choose female or BIPOC [Black, Indigenous, and People of Colour] owned), what products do you buy, who owns them, makes them, supplies them (consider the environmental and ethical implications), who do you contract for work in your home, who do you

give work to, who do you recommend, where are you investing your money, what is your pension linked to (choose ethical options, female/BIPOC led)?

8 **Your community** – where does inequity play out in your community, who can you support and mentor locally, where can you give money, time, volunteer your skills? What conversations can you start?

9 **National and international picture** – What causes, changes, movements do you want to be part of? Where can you lend your voice?

Use the following reflection point to consider how you can use your privilege as your superpower.

REFLECTION POINT

How can you use your privilege at work this week? Over the next month? Through this next year?

What access do you hold?

Where can you invite others in?

Who can you speak about, who's not in the room?

Whose work can you elevate? How can you use your privilege in your various spheres of influence?

How can you break into that positive spiral of privilege begetting privilege and *disrupt* it, interrupt the pattern and bring unexpected, new, fresh, others into the mix?

Whose contribution can you amplify?

How can you leverage all aspects of your privilege – your time, energy, money, access in your wider life and community?

What are you willing to invest in this work?

What may it cost you?

....

....

....

....

....

Think about your whole ecosystem of relationships, think about your Ikigai from Chapter 4 and your thriving visualization from Chapter 3. How can you leverage your connections for the benefit of others who hold less privilege than you, and for increased liberation, healing and freedom?

DISMANTLING AND DISRUPTING, RATHER THAN RESCUING

Our job when we have privilege is not to rescue others but to dismantle the systems that oppress others. We're invited to disrupt the systems where we hold power. This can actually be harder, right?

It may feel easier to be the 'rescuer' rather than the 'dismantler'. The rescuer receives the strokes of feeling needed, wanted, of being obviously useful. It's a way of retaining power.[37] The dismantler is a disruptor. It's about a giving away or a reallocation of power. You're charting new territory, breaking new ground, you play a more unsettling role. What you're doing is counter-cultural, you're speaking truth to power, you may be rejected. It can be easier to see how to be the rescuer (e.g. give money); it can be more complex to see how to be the dismantler.

JUST START

This work is still 'in progress' for me! I've invested in supervision, coaching, therapy, paid programmes, reading and personal study. And I realize how much I still need to learn and grow. So, patience and persistence with yourself here!

And the realization that you've some way to go, and that there may be some work and investment involved, is not a reason not to start.

THERE MAY BE A FEW DIFFERENT DYNAMICS AT PLAY FOR YOU HERE – WHICH DO YOU RECOGNIZE?

First, as women we tend to want to have everything ready and we tend to want to be prepared,[38] and this can lead to us holding back, playing smaller, waiting and remaining quiet, because we don't feel ready. This is a tool of the system to reduce our power – start anyway!

Second, disrupting the system is all about power! If we hold power and privilege in a particular system, we may tend to prioritize our own comfort, or fear of discomfort, over the safety and seeking of justice for others.

Third, from a psychological perspective, when anything seems hard we tend to resist and move away. It takes focus and intentionality to keep going when things get tricky! You're going to need a strong compelling 'why' to support yourself to keep going. Dig into your power practices, come back to your purpose for being part of this change-making work.

Notice if you're tempted to start and then give up; perhaps you recognize that you've had bursts of energy that have dissipated. We can't all give attention to everything, and we each make choices about where we place our time, attention, efforts, money and so on (and you'll remember that in Chapter 5 I encourage you to focus rather than dissipate your energies!). Also notice that it's part of our privilege that we can 'park' this work, 'take a break' or avoid doing the work altogether.

Fourth, fear of failure and fear of messing up. We may want to get this right, not offend anyone. But we *will* make mistakes, and it's better that we get really good at sincerely apologizing, choosing learning and determining to do better than that we stay silent and choose not to step into this aspect of our change making. Silence is complicity and complicity causes harm. Remind yourself of growth mindset from Chapter 2.

In Chapter 7 we'll look at getting visible and using the power of our relationships and collaborations, so that we're stronger together.

SOME OVERALL REFLECTIONS AND NOTES ON THIS ASPECT OF OUR CHANGE-MAKING WORK

1 It's on us to educate ourselves.
2 If we hold privilege in a system, it's on us to dismantle it, not on those who are disadvantaged by it.
3 Pay those who educate us. Don't expect those with a different identity to yours to labour for free to help you grow in your understanding and become a better human. Where you've received value, where you've grown and learned, let that be reciprocal and pay for that labour which supported you on your journey.
4 We're shifting from bystander to active challenger and co-creator.[39]

5 We *will* make mistakes. If we're learning and growing in our work to create more equitable organizations, and in our anti-racism work, we need to be ready to (as Erica Hines reportedly says) 'be humble and ready to fumble'. We need to get really good at trying, at going again, at digging deep into our growth mindset: 'Ok I messed up, I'm learning, now how can I do better?'

6 Shame isn't helpful. We can feel humiliated or distressed when we become conscious of wrong behaviour – we're in threat response and that can lead us to denial or causing more harm, as opposed to encouraging us to face up to our behaviours. Feeling guilt or empathy can lead us to reflect on our actions and words, take responsibility, and this leads to changes in behaviours. Let's not stay in shame or aim to shame others. Let's keep choosing compassion, curiosity and growth mindset, and invite others to join us.

7 Keep digging into joy, hope, pleasure, as fuel for your change-making journey. More coming in Chapters 7 and 8!

8 The pain of these experiences is real. The impacts of oppressions and the ways systems have held particular people and groups back are deep and long-lasting. New research suggests that trauma is stored in our DNA, at a cellular level, so we inherit generational trauma from our ancestors, further impacting our own lived experiences and sense of wellbeing.[40] If you've experienced systems and/or generational trauma, then just working on your mindset is unlikely to be enough to 'snap you out of it'. Tune into your body wisdom, know that you're worthy of healing and wholeness. Do access support available.

Health warning

If you're in a toxic, damaging workplace, where you don't feel psychologically safe and allowed to thrive, find ways to make it better; if that's not possible (we often stay longer and put up with more than we need to!), find a way to quit and what else you can change around you to make that happen. Find support, find allies, talk to your managers, find a coach, therapist or good friend with whom you can be accountable and who'll support you to make those shifts. Get together with others who want to see similar change in your workplace – find your Ikigai buddies! Create or find a workplace culture that'll allow you to thrive, where you can feel psychologically safe and can contribute to the safety, wellbeing and thriving of others.

Unwind rewind: chapter summary

We've covered a lot in this chapter! We've explored some key systemic factors where we need to dial up our awareness and navigate as change makers, as we step up, and if we want to avoid burning out!

I trust that you can now say 'I've got "the glasses on", I can see how bias and conditioning are shaping so much of the systems that I'm navigating'. That you can see how you are in the system and the system is in you, that you can choose to unlearn and relearn. This awareness gives you more choice in your thinking and change-making actions. I trust that you can now identify the privilege you carry with curiosity and awareness, rather than getting stuck in guilt or shame. You can see where headwinds and tailwinds have helped (and hindered) you in your workplace and your career, and their impact on others. I trust you can alchemize your privilege into a superpower and feel inspired to elevate and amplify others. When you know better, you can do better!

In Chapter 7 we'll dial up your change-making impact via your visibility and your ecosystem of relationships.

UNWIND REWIND

What's most important for you from this chapter?
What will you experiment with?

YOUR CHANGE-MAKER PROGRESS + ACTION TRACKER

- This is the action I'm taking to make a difference.

- This is what I'm experimenting with.

- This is what I'm noticing.

AFFIRMATIONS

'I choose to unlearn and relearn.'
'I rise up.'
'I lift as I climb.'
'Together we rise.'
'There's more than enough for all of us.'

'We can make bigger tables.'

'We are each and all welcome.'

'Wherever I am, I belong' (thanks to Sima Kumar for this one).

CHANGE MAKER INTERVIEW   Mireille Harper

Mireille Harper *is an award-winning editor, writer, sensitivity reader and communications consultant, featured in* British Vogue, *Digital Spy,* Good Housekeeping, *Nation of Billions, GUAP,* Nataal *and* TOKEN Magazine, *and consulting with Punch Records, BYP Network, ShoutOut Network and other organizations. Mireille is a contributor to* Timelines of Everyone, The Black History Book *and* Migrations *and the author of* Timelines from Black History. *Her essay 'Why Passivity Will No Longer Do' is published in Feminist Book Society's anthology,* This Is How We Come Back Stronger.

I talked with Mireille about her change making in the publishing industry, how she stays resilient and overcomes barriers.

I'm a change maker because I've used my knowledge and lived experiences to change processes and attitudes in the industries I'm in.

My route into publishing wasn't traditional – since the age of 16 I'd worked across retail, visual merchandising, customer service and had work experience placements in a range of industries while teaching myself PR and social media, so I approach a lot of what I do with my various experiences in mind. As well as this, I've worked in diversity and inclusion (D&I) organizations and charitable, grassroots and community interest companies (CICs) since I was a teenager, so I've always felt the need to apply outreach and giving to the working environments

I'm in. I think having this holistic overview of how other organizations work has proved immensely useful for me in my career. Equally, having been a writer for eight years and now an author, I can see the process of publishing a book from the other side, which is incredibly useful for me when navigating my own relationships with authors.

On resilience

Resilience to me is existing and surviving despite the odds. Growing up as a second-generation immigrant in the UK, resilience is close to home. Both my grandmothers were immigrants – one from Germany and the other from Jamaica. Both, at various points in their lives, were single mothers, and both endured xenophobia, discrimination and prejudice. They both worked hard to own their own homes, established careers for themselves and carried on, no matter what life threw at them. Whenever I am faced with challenges, I try to remember that their strength and resilience lie within me.

I've had my fair share of ups and downs in the Covid pandemic, and my resilience has been tested on many accounts. I've tried to maintain my positivity, but I've also allowed myself to go through the motions emotionally, take time off to heal where necessary and engage in acts that bring me joy. Copious amounts of chocolate, wine, cups of tea and takeaways have also assisted in me staying resilient.

On finding your change-making contribution

I think it's about channelling what makes you feel evoked emotionally. Whether that's something that makes you feel so happy you might burst or so angry that it keeps you up at night, it's finding the thing that affects you on an emotional level and makes you want to get up and do something. I don't actually believe you have to be an expert or you need to have been involved for years to be able to add a contribution or to be a voice, but I do think it's worth seeing what ecosystems, infrastructures and voices are already involved in what you consider to be your purpose. Finding what is already in place can help you establish how you connect more, contribute to the conversation and lend your voice.

On support and collaboration

I'm lucky to have a lot of good friends who work in the same or similar industries who I can bounce off ideas with, seek support from and vent to when things get too much. I'm also fortunate to have friends who check in to ensure I'm not overworking and that I'm taking time for me. I also have an accountability partner – my best friend whom I've known since I was four days old – and we set ourselves relevant goals, checking in regularly to see how the other is getting along. I can't describe how vital it is to have a support network around you – whether it's accountability partners, hype people or just solid friends.

I think it's impossible to make tangible and large-scale change without collaboration, and I think change making is about collaborating and connecting with those who can help you on that journey. In my life, I think I take a collaborative approach to most things.

On navigating bias in your sector of publishing

My experience of navigating 'the system' in the world of work has been interesting to say the least. Having worked across a range of industries since I was a teenager, I've mastered the art of navigating the spaces I'm in. I quickly work out whether I'm 'safe' or not, who my support network is going to be and I learn pretty fast what's going to work, what won't and how I can protect myself. I try to be as open as possible but also hypervigilant and prepared for what might arise.

It's very easy for people to place you in a box and see you as being able to exist only in one sphere, without realizing that you can be a multifaceted human being with a variety of interests.

Nowadays, I'm very clear and open – I clearly say when I don't understand the vocabulary some people are using, I ask people to break things down into layman's terms for me to understand what they are saying, as there's a lot of publishing jargon and ways of conversing that go over my head, and I use my cultural reference points and interests (from podcasts to TV shows) in the same way as my counterparts as a way of juxtaposing what is considered 'the norm'. With every workplace I've been in over the course of my career, I've established partnerships or outreach opportunities as I think this is a key way of bringing people in and reinforcing collaboration. Creating tangible or long-term change is not being the person that everyone recognizes or goes to as a spokesperson; it's about creating ecosystems, infrastructures and networks that multiple people can be a part of.

'If you can't get a seat at the table, build a new table'

I try to carry this mentality through all I do. I've established partnerships throughout my time in publishing from establishing long-term volunteering plans with social care organizations or committing to long-term book donation drives. I job share 50 per cent of my freelance opportunities and panel talk requests, both with those I don't know and those in my network who are just as, if not more, qualified to take them on.

On dealing with opposition to your change-making work

With any change making, you'll always face opposition. You're going against the grain and with that comes backlash or retaliation in one form or another. Especially if you're disrupting the status quo.

Some of the opposition is rooted in truth – how much time can I feasibly give to these projects? Do my notions of morality and ethics juxtapose the systems I'm trying to create change in? Is change really change if it exists within an exploitative and unequal system or society? These questions play on my mind incessantly.

My way of dealing with it is to figure out if what I'm doing might impact me emotionally, mentally and physically. I assess my priorities and my capacity, I look at who can support me and share the load, and I work out from there how to proceed.

What do you see is the future of work and/or your dream future workplace, such that it meets people's needs?

I hope that workplaces will just be more flexible, open, supportive of different styles of working and more collaborative with other industries and organizations.

CHAPTER SEVEN

Change-making ecosystem

Dialling up your visibility

Find a group of people who challenge and inspire you, spend a lot of time with them, and it will change your life. AMY POEHLER[1]

You've examined your privilege. You're switched on to injustices in your workplace. You want to be part of making a positive change and you know what's your *yes*! So now what?

We can't solve world and workplace inequities through personal development alone. We need to do the work as individuals, but we also need to work collectively.

This chapter is all about boosting your change-making ecosystem with alliances, collaborations and visibility!

Building on our previous chapters where we've strengthened your inner dialogue and your personal and systems awareness, this chapter enables you to dial up your brilliance and shine even more brightly.

In Part 1 we'll explore **Visibility and you** – why it's important, why it's so hard and how we make it safer. As women we're socialized that we need to compete rather than collaborate, with beliefs running about there not being 'enough' (e.g. opportunity, roles, money, etc). This underpins competitive behaviours as well as comparison and imposter syndrome. We'll look at how you can handle these dynamics and you'll create a visibility manifesto.

In Part 2 we'll explore the question 'can I really meet the Obamas?' By mapping, extending and **turbo-charging your personal change-making ecosystem,** finding and connecting with cheerleaders and role models, you'll create your own ecosystem map.

In Part 3 we'll explore how **support plus accountability is magic** for us as change makers. You'll map your collaborators and alliances. It's not all rose-tinted and we'll dig into the pain of professional break ups, break downs and how we can recover.

Visibility

If you've a sense of bigger purpose, if you've a sense of your identity as a change maker and what's possible, then you need to contend with getting visible – it's going to be part of it! Visibility plays a key role in our progression inside an organization, in the industries and sectors that we work within. If others can't see your brilliant work, they'll not gain the benefits of it – you're depriving them of your brilliance! In this section we explore visibility, how we can do it more easily and with whom.

Inside organizations, your visibility impacts your access to promotion, stretch assignments and further development.[2] We need and want more women and people with marginalized identities in senior positions, influencing across all sectors. A quick word about representation here – which is the idea that we 'need to see it so we can be it'. When women with multiple intersections of their identity 'make it' to visible roles, it opens up others' possibility thinking: 'if they can do it, so can I'. We need people who'll not only navigate the system for their own access, and to be role models for others, but also use their privilege to re-create and dismantle for the benefit of others. So, it's in all our interests to get really good at our own visibility and opening up spaces for others to shine.

If you're running your own business or change-making initiative, visibility is *essential* to get your brilliant work 'out there', for those who need to see it and benefit!

Why visibility can feel unsafe or tricky to navigate

You playing small and holding back your voice and visibility may feel like that's the best option, and it's understandable – we've stayed safe by remaining under the radar and not standing out, people pleasing and fulfilling others' stereotypical expectations. There's a huge cost to this. We bend ourselves out of shape to fit in, deny or minimize our own desires and dreams, and withhold from the world the change-making impact we could bring.

Being visible in the workplace doesn't feel safe for all of us. In Chapter 6 we explored the impact of microaggressions and bias playing out in workplaces, how important psychological safety is, and how to create more of it for yourself, your teams and those you lead. We explored how bias plays out and impacts us as women. We're socialized not to be 'too big for our boots', not to be the tall poppy and not to stand out for fear of being rejected.[3] We don't learn in school how to self-promote in a natural and ease-filled way.[4] The double bind we explored in Chapter 6 means we're judged as less likeable if we're 'too strong' and also as less competent if we don't exhibit strength – it's a tricky one to navigate!

Women are spoken over, interrupted more, and take less airtime than men in meetings,[5] although people (all genders) think women take up more than they do. Numerous studies have shown how women are taken less seriously.[6]

At the same time, we're socialized that we need to compete rather than collaborate, with beliefs running about there not being enough (e.g. opportunity, roles, money, etc). This feeds into our comparison spikes and our sense of being an imposter.

We're encouraged to believe that we have imposter syndrome, feeling we're undeserving of our achievements, or not as competent or intelligent as others think we are, that we're a fraud, even if there's abundant evidence to the contrary, and sooner or later they'll find out! Yes, we need to do our inner work to build our resilience and healthy mental habits, *but* often, we're labelling something 'imposter syndrome' as a way to make it about fixing women, when it's actually about the system.[7] We position imposter syndrome as if there's something wrong with us, or broken, when we're actually experiencing systemic barriers (or headwinds as we explored in Chapter 6).

Change makers talked to me not about doubting themselves ('I know I'm not fake, I know I'm competent') but about doubting the safety of the work environments they were part of and the support and advocacy available from managers and colleagues. Once again, when we hold privilege and power in a system, it's on us to do the work to make it safer for others!

There's extra 'visibility vulnerability' if we're the first woman with a particular characteristic to hold a position of senior leadership. Amanda Khozi Mukwashi talks about the energy it takes to justify your existence at the top, the expectation to continually over-perform and the subsequent impact on retention she notices for women of colour particularly.[8] She credits her wider sisterhood of women who've lifted her and sustained her.[9] Leyla Hussein told me how this visibility vulnerability extends beyond one's current role: 'being a Black woman when we reach a certain point (in our career progression), there can be a fear of where can we go now, can I even leave, will I get this opportunity again?'

Our society and dominant culture have obsessive focus on women's outward appearance, with very specific beauty standards that encourage us to judge ourselves and others, to minimize and censor ourselves, while also rendering whole swathes of our society invisible.

All these factors combine to create conditions where it can feel tricky to be visible.

REFLECTION POINT

What thoughts and feelings come up for you when we talk about visibility here? Tune into your inner dialogue as we practised in Chapter 2.

Do you feel safe to become more visible? If so, what's enabling that? If not, what's that about for you?

How can you dial up your safety to become more visible? What support do you need to build your resilience with this?

....
....
....
....
....

As we explored in Chapters 1 and 2, we learn to feel safe by tending to our central nervous systems. We can also ally with others to co-create more psychologically safe workplaces! Again, it's inner and outer work, personal and system.

When comparison strikes, when our inner critic is dialled up loud, judging ourselves as in deficit compared to other women, when we can feel the pressure to conform to societal or workplace culture expectations, when we can feel the headwind we're running against: here's a reminder that we're experiencing part of the *system*.

And our role if we have privilege in the system... is to dismantle it!

So, dial up your inner wisdom, get your systems glasses on and let's go!

Judging other women

Notice when *you* judge other women for being too X, Y or Z (loud, pretty, out there, visible), notice when you react with 'how dare she seek attention!' or 'who do you think you are?!' Notice when you react with competitive behaviours, when you slip into comparison, or desire to put another woman down to put yourself in a 'better' light. Use the following reflection point to help you.

We're colluding with patriarchy when we choose to be part of this.

REFLECTION POINT

How do you judge other women?

How do you respond when other women are visible?

What about others' appearance, behaviours, actions, voice, mannerisms and ways of doing things brings out your 'judgey'?

How do you feel about this?

....
....
....
....
....

Disrupting imposter syndrome and comparisonitis

1 **Notice it's happening.** This awareness is the most important part!

2 **Interrupt**. Interrupt your pattern. Stand up, move around, if you're on your phone stop the scroll, look away to get a different focal length. Use your micro-resilience power practice (Chapter 3).

3 **Tune into your inner dialogue.** Use your noticing inner critic and inner wisdom (Chapter 2) to listen to what your inner dialogue's saying. Notice any thinking errors (Chapter 1).

4 **Reset.** Take a break. Come back to your reality, reconnect with your body. Reset your nervous system. Use your breathing and gratitude power practices (Chapter 1).

5 **Remember you're experiencing the system!** You are not broken.

6 **Recognize that you can take up your space.** You don't have to be somebody else. You don't have to be the expert or the 'best'. You're entitled to your own interpretation. If you're feeling out of your depth, it's a sign that you're pushing yourself and stretching to new territory!

7 **It's ok not to know** – you can find out later. Saying 'I don't know' and/or 'I'll get back to you'[10] demonstrates you're willing and open to learn.

8 **Reconnect with your goals.** Reconnect with *your* values and what's most important to *you*. Why are you doing what you're doing? Use this opportunity to re-clarify your 'yes' and refocus on your purpose (Chapter 4).

9 **Find your allies, collaborators and sisterhood.** More below.

10 **Keep showing up for your work:** small steps every day, use your intention-setting power practice (Chapter 3), reviewing progress and weekly wins power practice (Chapter 5).

11 **Dial up your self-care**, refresh your resilience map and refocus your morning routine (Chapter 3).

12 **Use your affirmations** to remember who you are! See the list at the end of each chapter and the full list at my site, www.katycatalyst.com/change-makers-book.

13 **Love others.** Use your voice, amplify others, be generous in your giving, pay it forward.

Don't follow what anyone else is doing, especially within your own space. It will drive you crazy! (Lara Sheldrake)

Ok, back to visibility!

Here's the thing... *We don't have to be visible to everyone.*

We have to be visible to those who can help us, or who can benefit from what we do. Tapping into this wider vision of why we need and want to be visible can help us get over any awkwardness or holding back.

HOW DO WE GET COMFORTABLE WITH GETTING VISIBLE?

1 **Breathe** always! Connect with your body, soothe your threat response, know that you're safe in this moment.

2 **Connect with your goals**. What's the bigger picture for you, why is it important to you? Feel the resonance of that full-body *yes*. Who are you serving, whose lives will you impact? Use your thriving visualization from Chapter 3.

3 **Map out your visibility stakeholders**. Whom do you want to reach and where are they? Where are your allies and co-workers, whom can you amplify?

4 **Make a plan.** How can you help each other to feel safer in your change-making work? What practical support and accountability can you offer and receive?

ON THE ONE HAND... IT'S NOT ABOUT YOU

It's about your work, your community, clients and beneficiaries, the impact you want to have in your change making.

ON THE OTHER HAND... IT IS ABOUT YOU

You don't have to do visibility like everyone else. You can be you! What communication methods do you prefer? Writing, spoken word, video? Use a methodology that suits you best. You get to choose. Do you like to prepare ahead or riff on the day? You choose. Back to our seasons and cycles: visibility is your Summer energy; you'll get exhausted if you're always 'ON'. How can you build in each season to support your increased visibility, particularly the energy of Autumn and Winter? How does your best future self in your visualization from Chapter 3 do visibility? How can you access your creativity, your joy and even have fun?

WHAT IF IT JUST DOESN'T FEEL SAFE TO GET VISIBLE?

Can you get out? You have one unique and precious life, you are valuable, you have so much to give, so don't stay somewhere where you're boxed in and unappreciated. Don't stay somewhere where your light isn't able to shine. Talk to others, talk to your boss, ask for what you need. If you've expressed your needs and you realize they can't be met, that's useful data for you. Start looking elsewhere. If trauma is triggered, seek help from a qualified clinician.

MANIFESTO

Let's...

Reclaim visibility and find ways to do it that feel good.

Stop doing patriarchy's job, let's stop judging other women.

Model what healthy self-promotion looks and feels like.

Get support as we do this; it's baby steps and it can feel wobbly as we strengthen our muscles here.

Make it safe for others to do it in their way too – this is part of creating a team environment which is psychologically safe for others.

Champion others in their visibility, speak about them, cheerlead, share their work.

What more can you add to this visibility manifesto?

Turbo-charging your relationship ecosystem

In this section we're discussing how we can turbo-charge our network and 'pay it forward', who we create access for, and how we can be a role model for others, with the premise that we cannot be what we cannot see.

The big issues that you're tackling in your workplace and world of business are not pieces to do alone – our change making doesn't happen in isolation; this work is collaborative and who else we're connected with matters.

Who's in your network of change makers? Who do you have on speed dial?

Who are the mentors, role models, co-conspirators, supporters, funders, friends, colleagues... inside and outside your organization? Who can you call when you're struggling, despondent or exhilarated?

As you're chipping away at your place in the wall, who do you look up to see what they're doing and it boosts you, inspires you?

If you can't yet answer these questions, this section will help you to identify, find and connect with those people. Your ecosystem is simply your connections, your relationships. In this section we'll get savvy about how you can grow, stay connected with and maximize your ecosystem.

We're far more powerful in our togetherness. I'm inspired by Deepa Iyer's work where she encourages us to find our people, acknowledge the different roles we can play and find our place within that.[11] When you find other people who care about the cause, injustice or change that you care about, you can join forces, ask how you can help, how you can get involved, ask what they've learned so far.

If we hold privilege, we can choose to listen and follow, not lead!

We also know that social change ecosystems are themselves prone to maintaining cultures of overwork, productivity and performance at the cost of individual wellbeing and long-term sustainability. Developing our ecosystems is one way we can resource ourselves and support ourselves in the work. We can also consider how our ecosystem can create conditions for justice, liberation, inclusion, solidarity. What are we modelling to others? (See Chapter 3 for other ways to boost your wellbeing and sustainability!)

Don't wait till you need something before you start building your ecosystem

People I've known for 20 years, 2 years or 2 months call on me, and I on them. I 'pay it forward' in my networks of consultants and I offer tangible help where I can – sharing work opportunities, connections, ideas, resources, actively cheerleading others' work, their offers and promotions, boosting others' visibility. I give attention to my ecosystem, keeping in touch with people on email, text, voice note, or sending resources: 'I saw this and thought of you'. I do this because it gives me joy! And also, so that when I have an 'ask' in the future, or when I need support, the relationships are built and building.

Building your ecosystem is essential for:

- your visibility and audience building;
- your progression and promotional opportunities (women who form a strong inner circle with other women and share career advice are three times more likely to

get a better job than women who don't have that support system);[12]

- your resilience and wellbeing;
- your effectiveness – being alongside others: having co-conspirators in your change-making work is more fun, energizing and ultimately more sustainable than doing it alone.

Create your ecosystem map

Create a chart like the template at Table 7.1 and map out your ecosystem of relationships.

TABLE 7.1   Map your ecosystem

	Personal	Day-to-day	Strategic
Inside your current organization			
Outside your current organization			

Personal is for people who support and help you, including friendships. **Day-to-day** is for people who help you get work stuff done. **Strategic** focuses on the future: people who help you engage with the bigger picture for your industry, sector, area of work and change making.[13]

Who goes where? Name the individuals.

Now zoom out and take a look at your map.

Do you have any gaps?

Does your ecosystem reflect your past self, your current self, your future self?

Breaking out of your echo chamber

Because of the way that affinity bias works (see Chapter 6), we tend to move towards people like us and be drawn to work with and build friendships with people like us: people who look similar, come from similar backgrounds, hold similar perspectives and social status indicators. We create our own in-groups, our own bubbles, and this 'echo chamber' effect is exacerbated by social media as the algorithm feeds us more of the same.

Think about the five people you spend most time with – at work, in your change making, in your personal life. How much do they look like you? How similar to you are they? How are they different? (Reference your intersectionality map from Chapter 2.)

How diverse is your ecosystem? Multiple studies have shown that more diverse and connective ecosystems are stronger.[14] Consider age and stages of life, fields of expertise, background and professional expertise, values and life perspectives, lived experiences, socio-demographics. Where can you extend your connections, to break out of your 'bubble'?

> Yes, we need to see so we can be. I didn't know I could be a campaigner because I'd never seen one. So, I didn't even try till I was 27. In other respects, I knew I could speak out. I'm white, middle class and have a Cambridge degree and it never occurred to me that I wouldn't be listened to once I did decide to speak out. Now the people I'm learning most from are Black women campaigners and feminists. (Anthea Lawson)

Does your ecosystem reflect your best future self?

Think back to your thriving visualization from Chapter 3 (you're still practising it, right?!). Or even better, run the visualization again for yourself right now.

Ask these questions: who does she hang out with, who does she learn from, who does she surround herself with, who does she spend time with?

What insights does this give you as to what needs to change in your mix of relationships? Where can you extend your ecosystem?

STORY   Extending my ecosystem

A number of years ago I realized my professional ecosystem was a bubble of people who looked like me and represented all my previous jobs and clients, but not 'future me'. I knew I wanted to educate myself in intersectional feminism and go deeper in my equity and anti-racism work.

I decided to take some intentional action. I found a supervisor who was an older Black woman. I found and attended book launch events with Black women authors and leaders who I was listening to and learning from. I joined paid anti-racism education programmes and shifted my reading lists (and the kinds of programmes I binge-watched on Netflix!).

I left a system and network of consultants, even though they were supportive with lots of like-minded people. I chose to connect into female-centred groups that had younger, older, less white, less middle class and not just white women in the mix.

I sought out teams, collaborators, connections who looked different from me and had a wide variety of lived experiences. This has extended, deepened and enriched the work of the EDI consultancy I lead, as well as my personal life.

My professional ecosystem now looks really different after a slow, steady, intentional process of growing and developing these relationships.

You deserve to be championed

You, in all your brilliance, your perspectives, your fresh insights, your experiences, are bringing your *self* to your workplace. You deserve to be championed! Who's mentoring you, sponsoring you? Who are your role models and real models? Who champions and cheerleads for you?

Paying it forward

In Chapter 6 you examined your privilege and we talked about who you can sponsor, mentor, uplift and amplify.

As you look at your ecosystem and think about who's mentoring you and who your role models are, we can also flip this on its head. Who are *you* a role model for, who's looking to you for inspiration, solidarity, guidance? Without you necessarily even knowing, who's watching your life? There'll be more people than you think; you're quietly influencing more than you know! What you're doing, how you're showing up in the world, how you are *being* is enabling others to see what's possible for them.

Let's consider where and how we can 'pay it forward', who we can create access for, how you can be a role model for others.

> There's something to be said for cultivating an ability to clap for yourself, lead from the front and be your own cheerleader. Role models are important in modelling behaviour and demonstrating what's possible, but there comes a point where you have to be ready to pick up the baton and run in a direction that shapes a new reality for the next generation too. Sometimes we're our own best role models and we should take great comfort in that. (Davinia Tomlinson)
>
> We'll never see anyone doing 'it' quite like us, but that's ok. I like to focus on what I can learn from examples of someone's work or behaviour. A few times I've had people fall off the pedestals I've put them on, and while I love it when people tell me they admire my work, I know that breeds expectation. When a role model 'lets us down' (often just by being human!), it can feel like solid evidence that no-one is 'doing it right' or being authentic, and that can be hard to recover from. The more we learn, the more likely we are to be disappointed by others we've looked up to. (Keri Jarvis)

Support + accountability = magic for us as change makers

We're socialized as women to compete and compare, and the way we dismantle this system of oppression is through collaboration, reciprocity and alliances with others. Sisterhood and solidarity with others can feel problematic; we haven't learned how to do this, and our conditioning can get in the way. We're unlearning old patterns and need to be very intentional to set out new ways.

Support plus accountability is magic for us as change makers! We need spaces where we can be honest about the impact of our work, our needs, our desires, our challenges, failures, moments of hopelessness. We need spaces where we don't need to perform, be the leaders, the experts, the givers, where we can also receive and learn. We need spaces where we can be held accountable for our growth, our progress, our learning, where we'll be challenged. We need spaces where others are not intimidated by our brilliance, our ambition, or our power, and are genuinely invested in our flourishing.

So few leaders that I meet have these kinds of brave spaces where they can show up as 'work in progress', in all the messy mix of strength and vulnerability, rather than their perceived expectation that they have to have it all figured out.

If **you** are going to step up in your leadership and change-making work, as we've talked about throughout this book, you need this kind of support around you in your ecosystem. As a start-point, can you identify a person in your ecosystem that you can support and check in on regularly, and someone who can do the same for you? Use the following reflection point to help you.

REFLECTION POINT

What kind of support do you need around you to support you, and keep you accountable in your change making?

Where do you get your support – where you can feel deeply seen, heard, connected?

Where can you receive as well as give?

Where do you get your accountability? Do you receive enough challenge in your leadership?

How can you be intentional to find, create and sustain these kinds of connections?

What's your best next step?

....

....

....

....

....

Expanding and extending your ecosystem – how to find your people

If you want a particular kind of relationship or particular kind of friendship – set it up!

I'm very intentional in how I develop my ecosystem and relational village, recognizing that different people and different kinds of relationships meet different needs.

Here are some examples:

- I set up a friendship network in my community where we schedule dinner six times over the year as a way to stay connected with three other couples, when I was feeling isolated in my community and realizing I wanted to develop deeper friendships.

· I set up a girls' night for my fellow mums, when my kids were small, a space to chat and laugh together.
· I co-created a regular walk 'n' talk families meet-up, where we explore spirituality while enjoying being outside.
· I set up a mini-mentoring group for teen girls.
· I co-founded my current company and loved the collaborative energy of that partnership. When my cofounder left the business, there were aspects of what that relationship gave me that I wanted to re-create. I chose to foster new relationships that would enable me to be in that collaborative, creative, expansive energy.
· I set up an action learning group for myself with peers in consulting/OD/leadership development/coaching industries.
· I set up a business mastermind that's now become my change maker's mastermind.

I know this is my superpower! You'll have your own ways to create more of the kinds of relationships you desire.

Can I meet the Obamas?

There's an exercise I run in my leadership workshops, based on the theory that there's only 5–7 degrees of separation between us.[15] When you run this exercise in a room (even a Zoom or Teams room), it's amazing what resources and connections emerge, demonstrating how we have the potential to connect with whomever we want.

We start with the question 'who do you want to meet?' and then 'let's see if we can meet them!'

Oprah and Nelson Mandela used to come up, now it's always one of the Obamas – usually Michelle.

We ask: 'who do you know who you think may be connected in some way?' We start from who we know in the room and everyone contributes as we build up a flow chart.

Then 'who do you know who may know someone… who may know someone…?' Yes, there are some leaps ('well, I could contact her… and maybe she'd put me in touch with her connection at…)

I guarantee that, without fail, we find a way to connect with the Obamas. Every single time.

STORY   From intimidation to collaboration

Three years ago, I made a list of all the women I saw on my horizon (mostly on social media via Instagram and LinkedIn) with whom I wanted to connect. Women I admired, who I was a bit intimidated by, whose brilliance scared me a little, women I wanted to learn from and be around, whose energy and wisdom I wanted to soak up, noticing who I was drawn to, who I wanted to be challenged and boosted by. I also considered women whom I'd love to serve in some way, where I wanted to be part of their support and accountability ecosystem.

I listed them out by name and tucked that list away. A few months later, I found that list again and noticed my brain starting to think about how I could connect with each person.

When I looked at that list again recently, *every single woman* had come closer in my ecosystem of relationships. I'd helped them or they'd helped me in some way. I'd either directly met them, we'd collaborated, they were in my mastermind, I'd been a guest on their podcast, or I'd invited them to be part of this book. In some cases we'd talked once, shared some resources and that was it. In others we talked and have stayed in touch as friends. In one case I decided we probably wouldn't work together, but I find myself now referring clients to her and asking for advice on connections she has. Women who a couple of years back seemed out of reach or aloof strangers to me are now my peers and friends.

Once we get intentional, our brain starts working for us and finding ways. This is how serendipity works (that and the internet algorithm!). You want to buy an electric car and you start researching options, and suddenly you start seeing electric cars everywhere. I want to extend my ecosystem of awesome women, I set some intentions around it, my brain opens up my possibility thinking and I start to see opportunities for connection.

I now need a new list!

This is about e-x-p-a-n-d-i-n-g your capacity for connection. Use the following reflection point to help you.

REFLECTION POINT

Create your list of change-making inspirations.
Who do you want to learn from? Who can open some
    doors for you?

How do you want to grow by being connected?

Who would you like to support? What can you give? How can you amplify their change-making work?

....

....

....

....

....

Take it a stage further – allow your brain to show you ways you could connect with that person, or other connections that can connect you – it's like meeting the Obamas! See Table 7.2.

TABLE 7.2 Extend your ecosystem

Who do I want to meet?	Where are they?	Who do I know who could connect me?	Ideas to connect with them

Set aside time each week, or each month, to grow your ecosystem. Think back to your intention-setting power practice in Chapter 3; your 'one thing I want to progress today' could be:

- I'll reach out to X and ask to be a guest on her podcast.
- I'll connect with Y on LinkedIn and share my white paper with her.

Use your Ikigai from Chapter 4 to help you 'find your people'. Where you have your overlap of what you're curious about, what you're angry about and what you can offer – as you move towards that, you'll find others! As Holly Whelan, Founder of Younger Lives Limited said in my change-maker interviews, 'let's be individuals inspiring each other to achieve great things together'; this is all about reciprocal relationships and what you can add and build, to resource others.

Many women who're leaders can fall into the trap of mentoring and sponsoring others without receiving that in return. I find myself in this position quite often. The best support for me is conditional, generous, intersectional and honest.

My little corner of the internet is incredibly supportive – there are hundreds of women on there who've never even met me who celebrate my wins as much as their own and this means the world to me. This is immensely valuable to me and keeps me motivated.

My advice to anyone looking to build this support network would be to be patient. I've been trying and learning lessons the hard way for 13 years. People are inherently selfish, but symbiotic relationships work exceptionally well. This is the beauty of deeply honest networks.

The willingness to collaborate and share everything you know is a competitive advantage in work and life. Our power is our togetherness. (Lauren Currie)

When you're clear about what's your *yes* (see Chapters 4 and 5 to work on this) and you communicate that to your ecosystem, it becomes really easy for them to help you, refer to you, recommend you. This is how your ecosystem starts to work for you.

What happens when relationships move on

With many women I coach (and I include myself here) I notice a deep desire for intimacy, belonging and solidarity with other women. There can be a palpable experience of loneliness, even isolation, for women leaders.

Alongside that, many carry a fear of intimacy and connection, as a residue from past painful experiences. Many women are hurt by their relationships with other women and carry this pain.

My clients and my change-maker interviewees talk with me about these experiences. Going 'all in' when we do meet our kindred spirits, getting burned, experiencing disappointment, withdrawing and having that expectation or fear running and preventing us connecting at a deep level in the future. The experience through the Covid-19 pandemic of connecting across screens with hundreds, maybe even thousands, of people, and then experiencing the withdrawal and emptiness of lockdown.

Remember that we're conditioned for scarcity, competition, comparison, not for collaboration. It serves the system for us to be divided, and unskilled in collaboration and cheerleading for others. If we hold privilege in the system, our job is to dismantle the system and be part of co-creating something new. The sisterhood doesn't just happen without intentional healing work. We need to unlearn, release, forgive, relearn, rebuild.

Unwind rewind: chapter summary

In Chapter 7 we've explored visibility, how we can do it more easily and with whom, how we can turbo-charge our own ecosystems while also 'paying it forward', by considering who we create access for and how we can be role models for others, with the premise that we cannot be what we cannot see.

Building out from Chapter 6's discussion around competition and comparison, we've explored more about collaboration and alliances, proposing that support plus accountability is magic for us as change makers! You've completed your ecosystem map and identified how you can find your role models and cheerleaders.

In Chapter 8 we'll explore what happens if you can't get a seat at the table, what options are available to us when we feel we don't have access to the spaces of power, what it looks like to build 'new tables' and how we can be part of co-creating new systems.

UNWIND REWIND

What's most important for you from this chapter?

Have you found your people?

YOUR CHANGE-MAKER PROGRESS + ACTION TRACKER

- This is what I'm experimenting with.
- This is what I'm noticing.
- This is my best next step.

AFFIRMATIONS

'I am valuable.'

'I am capable, confident and creative.'

'I am stronger than I think….'

'My voice is clear and compelling, I use it to speak my truth.'

'It's safe for me to be visible.'

'It's safe for me to tell my own story.'

'I can find my people.'

'I lift as I climb.'

CHANGE MAKER INTERVIEW   Lara Sheldrake

Lara Sheldrake *is a speaker, mentor and founder of Found & Flourish, an online membership, media and events platform for women in business. Found & Flourish brand collaborations include Xero,* Startups Magazine, *Huckletree, PlusX, GA assembly, Mastercard and Penfold. Lara's been featured in* Forbes *and* Marie Claire, *and listed as one of the top 100 female business leaders across the UK 2020 as part of the f.Entrepreneur #ialso campaign. She's cited as one of the most influential female founders of 2020 by* Startups Magazine.

She's on a mission to make business accessible and less lonely for entrepreneurial women. After having her son and struggling with feelings of isolation, she decided to create the safe and nurturing space she craved when she was embarking on this new journey of motherhood and entrepreneurship. Through the power of community and collaboration, Found & Flourish empowers women to upskill, connect and truly flourish.

I talked with Lara about her change making, how she stays resilient, the role of collaboration and sisterhood.

I'm a change maker because I challenge the status quo and work tirelessly to create a safe space and platform for those who may otherwise be under-represented or overlooked. I'm passionate about women being equipped with the knowledge and confidence to launch and build impactful businesses, in a society where there's less oppression and where femininity is nurtured and encouraged within business. I'm building a business and platform that I wished I'd had access to when I set up my first business.

I want to create a safe and nurturing space where we leave our egos at the door and every single woman is invited to show up as their whole selves. We embrace differences and encourage a diverse school of thought.

On resilience

For me it's about feeling the fear, experiencing failure and not letting it deter you from the mission you're on. During the Covid-19 pandemic I've become more innovative, confident in my ability and aware of the true power of resilience within. The practices that help my resilience are reading, listening to podcasts, taking regular breaks and allowing myself headspace to do things that don't involve work or my laptop. Also kindness and forgiveness, something I never practised on myself but now it's the only way I get through the days. It's taken me three years to get here and I'm not sure there's any turning back! I work 4–5-hour days compared to the 18-hour days I used to work. This allows me time to recuperate, think creatively and plan my next move from a place of clarity rather than panic.

On finding your change-making contribution

Speak with people, have conversations with people who inspire you. Use your voice, it's the only way you learn how to refine it. Don't be afraid to speak out about the things that make you angry, or that you are passionate about. It's through this bravery that we discover who we really are and what gets us fired up and motivated each morning. Some people go their whole lives trying to fit in and as a result they miss the opportunity to discover themselves. Be brave enough to stand out, embrace your difference and identify what authenticity means to you. Being like everyone else is overrated!

On collaboration and sisterhood

I wouldn't be able to do anything I do without the collaborations and partnerships I've had over the years. From the content we provide to the events we host, everything has been in collaboration with others.

On navigating bias and barriers in the world of work

I was miserable working in the media industry (by the time I left). I felt I was in a monotonous rat race, managed by misogynistic men, many of whom were rude and completely disrespectful. I spent years working in misogynistic and sexist workplaces. Most of the time, due to naivety, I ignored it, but I eventually felt so exhausted I burned out and then left the corporate world forever.

It really put me off working at all for a while. I thought *'Is this it? Is this what I should be aiming for?'* I really lacked female role models during my time in the media industry, and the only female boss I had ended up having an affair with the CEO. It was a toxic environment where we were overworked and disrespected (even if the pay was relatively good compared to the industry standard).

Becoming my own boss was my way of being able to call the shots, earn the money I wanted to earn while working with people I liked on things that mattered to me, so that I felt I was having a real impact in the work I was doing, as well as working the hours I wanted to work, so I could have the lifestyle I wanted for both myself and my growing family.

CHAPTER EIGHT

Change-making impact

*Pulling it all together to build a change-making
life you love – stepping up without burning out*

> *Not everything that is faced can be changed;
> but nothing can be changed until it is faced.*
> JAMES BALDWIN[1]

This chapter is all about pulling the threads together. It
builds on the self-awareness, leadership and resilience
foundations from Chapters 1, 2 and 3, the full-body yes
and make-it-happen practicality of Chapters 4 and 5, the
systems awareness we unpacked in Chapter 6 and the
shine-brighter focus from Chapter 7.

We'll look at how we can influence change and be part
of dismantling systems at individual, team and systems

levels. We'll discuss the options available to us when we don't feel we've access to the spaces of power, how we can be part of co-creating new systems. I'll introduce you to my hope-o-meter and how we stay compassionate as change makers for the long haul.

This chapter will close with your 'aha's, takeaways and what next.

What does it look like to rethink the world of work?

> We want more than inclusion, inclusion is not enough. We don't wish to be included in a racist society. If we say no to hetero-patriarchy, we don't want to be assimilated into a misogynist and hetero-patriarchal society. If we say no to poverty, we don't want to contained by a capitalist structure that values profits more than human beings. Our notions of revolution need to be far more capacious![2]

In every human system, there are those with power, access and prestige and those who are oppressed by that system. We're operating in ableist, sexist, patriarchal, heteronormative, white-supremacist workplace systems that weren't designed for us and not created for our flourishing. It serves those in power for the perception to be that they're more talented, smarter, more deserving of those spaces. And to create systems that serve them and keep them in power.

Part of unlearning our own internalized oppression is realizing that this is a lie, that we deserve to be 'there', if we choose to be. And beyond that, that we deserve better! That we can re-create systems that do serve us and our needs. We don't want to just tweak an old broken system to make it better for those for whom it wasn't even designed. There are plenty of people who've managed to enter systems and dismantled precisely nothing.

The Covid-19 pandemic has shown us that we can and do make significant changes when we need to; where there were sufficient (economic and/or political) pressures, millions of people shifted from their office base to working from home within weeks.

There's a new way coming – we're on the cusp of it. We're rethinking ways of working and ways of being that suit all humans – and the planet – better. We can start to re-create systems. We're interconnected, so we need to think in interconnected and systemic ways about our lives and the impact we can have.[3] It takes intentionality. Let's dream! Let's take action!

Cathy Reay, a disabled writer based in the UK, speaks to this vision when she shares she's:

> so bored of the rhetoric around 'not enough disabled people work here' as if it's somehow our fault that your organization is ableist as hell. If you're a company owner, director, on a board, or in an HR department you've a duty to normalize talking about access needs with every single employee… to start a dialogue from the get-go and do your absolute best to make any accommodations required, preferably before we get there. 'The changes needed are too much' doesn't fly anymore. If you want a diverse workforce invest in it.[4]

Ali Carruthers-Illingworth shared with me 'the seeing can be visionary, so it's not here yet, but you can still see it' and when I asked Tamu Thomas about what we can re-imagine for the future, she shared:

> I'm experimenting, I'm exploring, I'm being really still. It's reimagining, it's remembering and re-membering. Our biology knows it. We've been conditioned to believe that we need to understand, that first we need to see the puzzle pieces. When I'm talking about reimagining I'm talking about feeling. We believe we need to see it – but more often than not we're seeing what we're feeling.

Complex systemic change

When we're working on workplace equity, social and environmental issues, issues to do with justice and making the world a better place, we're working with 'wicked' problems.[5] The changes needed are multifaceted, with multiple stakeholders needing to engage in multiple different ways, and requiring a complex, multifaceted, joined-up approach. We're not talking here about one quick fix (or we'd have solved all our workplace and the world's problems by now, right?).

I spoke with Dr Kate Simpson, MD of Wasafiri and creator of Systemcraft, who shared that 'complex problems present in non-intuitive ways, meaning that we need to take time to deeply understand what's going on, the cause, rather than just reacting to the symptoms, otherwise at best we'll have very little impact and more likely can make things worse'.

Remember you're a change maker!

We can think about change at an individual, team and systems level (Figure 8.1).

You're a catalyst! You can decide where your sphere of influence extends, and at what level you want to operate. When you act in your sphere of influence at individual or team level, it can have wider cultural, structural, systemic, even societal impacts. When your individual change making becomes collective, you tap into collective power. You have more power than you may think you do!

Some examples:

- Whose job is it to solve pay gaps? Just those affected? No! Men (and others who 'fit' majority culture), who hold privilege in workplace systems, step up! To close gender and ethnicity pay gaps, it's essential to support individual women and people of colour to do the inner work to feel confident to ask for pay rises, get more visible and access promotional opportunities. But that's not

FIGURE 8.1   Individual, team, system

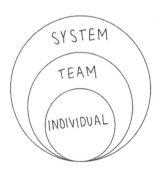

enough. It's also about managers supporting flexible working and shifting their biases around who they promote and amplify. At a team level, it's about creating psychologically safe workplaces and unpicking biases and barriers that exist for particular groups. At a workplace level, when women and men start to share what they're paid, levels of transparency increase and we know this contributes to closing pay gaps.[6] At a structural level, when organizations unpick their occupational segregation of who has which roles and what biases are running around recruitment, performance assessment and promotion, at a societal level when businesses are required to report on pay gaps, all these pieces play a part in bringing about the change we ultimately want to see.

- A woman is killed by a British police officer and there's a national outcry of both victim blaming and focus on how women can stay safe on the streets. It's essential to support women to feel safe, but that's not enough. There are cultural and procedural issues to address in the police force (cultural/systemic/structural level). It's also about the systemic violence and misogyny tolerated in British culture. The level of outcry from a majority white media and news agenda reveals their bias and another layer of British systemic racism is revealed. As white people start to feel unsafe with police, they experience something of the concerns that Black and Asian communities have been sharing for decades (systems, structure and societal level). Munroe Bergdorf writes 'to panic about receiving the same treatment as marginalized folks is rooted in privilege' and goes on to say 'I hope that within all these discussions, white cis het society starts to wake up to the fact that by centring the voices, experience and safety of most marginalized members of society, we are safeguarding the wellbeing of everyone'.[7]

- On suicide awareness day each year, we raise consciousness that it's essential to access therapy and mental health support, but that's not enough. It's also about systems and structures that people exist within, that contribute to suicidality – the impact of poverty, austerity cuts, debt and relationship strain, for example.

So how do we operate within these levels of individual–team–system? Step up and step in, use your voice!

Within your workplace and your organization, you can start conversations in your team. You can ask questions, ask for data, ask your senior leaders for change. We start with our own behaviours, modelling more of what we want to see and asking others to join us. Find a buddy for accountability and to help you keep up the momentum.

If we manage others, we start by having dialogue, asking for particular behaviours, keeping our team accountable and convening conversations to nudge those behaviours. We can talk to senior leaders, we can talk with HR, we can lend our support to employee resource groups, we can start one if they don't exist! We can keep the pressure up (systems love to 'snap back').

Within wider society we can vote, write to our MP, join campaigns, organize or join a march, stand for election. We can give money, donate items, volunteer, become trustees of charities for causes we care about. We can be selective about where we choose to spend, save and invest our money, discerning ethical and environmental considerations.

Let's investigate what it looks like to rethink the world of work.

Map your stakeholders

Who influences change in your workplace system? Who holds that power?

Kate Simpson emphasizes that the system is always working. 'The question is who and what it's working for. When we say "the system is broken" we become blind to the power in it – when you work out what and who it's working for, you've usually found the power in it.'

Have a think about your stakeholders. Where's their start-point (in terms of willingness or openness to the change you want to see, as well as in terms of power and influence that they hold), and where'd you like them to shift. You can also map out their specific interests, motivations and desires. If you don't know, be aware that you're working with assumptions. It's a way into a great conversation, to find out more!

How can you get visible in front of this group of stakeholders? How do you build relationships with those in power, and get them on board with your change? Who do you know, who can get you access? Back to your ecosystem mapping (Chapter 7).

We all have a role to play

In my EDI consulting work I spend significant time with senior teams and they're often majority white, male, cis and straight (or at least straight passing), able-bodied and neurotypical spaces. It can feel like I'm spending so much time nudging and influencing resistant middle-aged white men, so when (some of) those men 'get it' and show humility in their willingness to listen to others' lived experiences, then start to show up as sponsors, mentors, allies, it is so powerful and things start to shift at a cultural and systemic level.[8]

This is why we **each and all of us have a part to play** in bringing down the wall. We can each chip away. We each can show up in our own sphere of influence. Where we hold privilege, we can use it to dismantle systems.

Where we hold privilege, that's where we use our voice, we speak up, we can challenge the structures of power. Allyship is about joining with others on issues that don't necessarily directly impact us. All are welcome (don't try to lead, you need to show up *and follow*).

We all benefit!

Gender pay gaps, flexible working, access to affordable childcare and maternity rights – men speak up. Ethnicity pay gaps – white people speak up. LGBTQ+ rights – cis and straight people speak up. Disability rights and access – able-bodied folks, speak up!

STORY Developing my empathy

The frustration that white women experience when men don't step up, or use their privilege on causes that affect us, can give us just a small insight into the frustration that women of colour feel when white women don't step up or use their privilege, or how when they're in the system, accepted in the system, they don't dismantle anything.

When I started exploring my whiteness in my anti-racism journey, despite robust evidence points, I found multiple ways to resist and avoid; part of my privilege was that I could choose to look away and give my attention to something else. Knowing this about my own journey has given me (a little!) more empathy and willingness to go at the pace that others need, bringing more grace, compassion, patience....

When I'm frustrated at the pace of change in many male-dominated systems where I consult, or feel rage and frustration – 'why don't they just get it?!' or 'read the research!', I try to remind myself of the journeys that I've needed to make and the need to dig into growth mindset for the compassion and empathy that helps us progress.

And this ripples out into society's wider structural and systemic issues. Violence against women and girls – men, instead of 'not all-ing', speak up about toxic masculinity and model inclusive leadership! Abortion rights – men, speak up please, you also benefit from women's reproductive healthcare. Climate crisis – we *all* have a role to play and essential actions to take.

What to do about resistance

Do we need to engage everybody in our change making? Yes and no.

It's good to know where the resistance is, who it comes from and what's driving it. Kate Simpson reminds us that the resistance to change usually 'lies not in the things that aren't working, but in the things that are working'. What's working for those who hold power and privilege? This is useful data and insight for you as you plan your strategy, tactics, engagement and communications.

But do you need to put in loads of energy convincing people? I think no. Do you need to wait or halt your change-making work until all the resisters are fully on board? I think definitely no.

Nudges to help make change sustainable

As humans we're creatures of habit and we'll easily and quickly 'snap back' into what we know and what feels most familiar. Shifting into new behaviours can feel hard. In my experience, working on systemic change inside organizations, managers and leaders need nudges. Maybe you and members of your sisterhood can be part of the community of nudgers!

We'd worked inside a male-dominated system for two years. A senior leader shared with us how he felt when he first explored his own bias and saw the data about micro-aggressions in his part of the business: 'I didn't see it, I didn't believe it, I thought it must be somewhere else, not here, that's not who we are! Now I've understood that it goes on, and just because I don't see it, doesn't mean it's not happening. I've also seen how I've perpetuated non-inclusive cultures. Now I *really* see it!'

He's examining his privilege, changing up how he recruits people to bring more diverse candidates into his team, and he's engaging his team in how they together can create a psychologically safe team culture for everyone.

Amazing shift! *And* this man had multiple touchpoints and consistent nudges over two years – this is what it may take!

If we can't get a seat at the table

What are the options available to us when we feel we don't have access to the spaces of power?

You may feel like you can't, or don't want to, get a seat at the table of power in your particular organization. Maybe the doors seem firmly closed, or barriers and headwinds seem too strong.

You may have realized just how toxic your workplace situation is. You've tried to change it from the inside and experienced its intractability, and you've realized it's no longer sustainable for you to be there. Maybe you're choosing to walk away?

Back to Dr Leyla Hussein:

If you're struggling to stay resilient in your workplace, if the prevailing dominant culture is so strong, what's my advice? Each individual will be different. Check the level of toxicity. If you feel this is so toxic you can't even function, I would say leave.

However, I learned to build my allies, who don't work in the same workplaces as me, to help me stay. As an example, a friend of mine recently set up a specific WhatsApp group just for African feminist CEOs – all of us work separately, but what we're sharing helps us feel less alone, 'it's not just me'! Find your people where you share similar views, values and beliefs. You can feel lonely when you're the only one feeling like this. If that doesn't work – you can leave, you have the choice.

You may feel inspired, or compelled, to build a 'new table' or be part of co-creating new systems. I spoke with Roianne Nedd, an EDI leader and Founder of Trusted Black Girl, who shared: 'I'm always creating the tables I want to sit at, not because I can't always get a seat, but sometimes because the shape of the table doesn't suit me.' Lauren Currie shares that she doesn't accept the premise that she (or anyone else) can't get a seat at the table. 'I encourage us all to sit there no matter how uncomfortable it is, and no matter how hard it is to get a seat. When we get there, we make space for others and ruin dinner if we have to. We need to engage with everyone and have a dialogue around the table.'

Introducing your hope-o-meter

How we stay hopeful and keep our momentum going as change makers and workplace activists is so important. It can be near-impossible to stay compassionate when we're tired or close to burned out ourselves. I'm not talking about pushing through or denying our feelings. This is the balance of rest, joy, investing in our wellbeing.

You can imagine your levels of hope like a speed dial. My hope-o-meter fluctuates, I'll be honest! Some days (or moments of days) are a slog. Some days are easy speedy.

The issues we're addressing in our systemic change making can feel so entrenched, so overwhelming, so big. Often the clients I work with are looking to find their space, to know what they can do to make a difference. You may, to use our analogy from the Introduction, know you're at the wall, you're chipping away. But sometimes it can feel overwhelming, lonely, energy sapping. Sometimes it's about *sustaining* your space and keeping going over time. How do we deal with the burden and level of energy needed?

Check in with your hope-o-meter – how are you doing?! What practices can you do that you know will give you a boost?

I trust this book is helpful to boost your hope, and give you methods and ways to navigate the fluctuations in your hope-o-meter!

Find the place and be realistic about where you can make your difference (back to Chapters 4 and 5), sustain your wellbeing and resilience along the way (Chapters 3 and 7), just take the next best step.

> The world as I would like it to be needs me to be powerful. The systems of oppression benefit from me being disempowered. I choose to disengage from what makes me feel powerless. I focus on where I can be powerful and make change. (Tamu Thomas)

How to respond to energy-sapping hope dampeners

These narratives – in my own inner dialogue, or coming at me from others – can dampen my hope-o-meter. Which do you recognize? As well as dialling up my inner wisdom (Chapter 2) so I can hear her clarity and receive her sustenance, here's how I deal with these narratives.

'Things are getting worse, not better!'

It can often seem that way and with the pace of change and instantaneous news feeds giving us up-to-the-minute (heart) breaking news, it can feel like we're drip-fed continuous devastation and destruction. It can often feel like things are getting worse, before they get better. In my experience working as a consultant around diversity, equity and inclusion, when the 'glasses go on' inside organizations (see Chapter 6), and the light starts shining, some dark things can surface that start to be seen.

It's an unveiling, a revealing that has to come first. Shifting from unawareness and denial into awareness is deeply discomforting. I remind myself (and my clients) of James Baldwin's wisdom that started this chapter and Maya Angelou's encouragement that when we know better, we can do better. I hold on to the belief that the overall arc of history is bending towards justice[9] and that we're part of the tipping point![10]

REFLECTION POINT

What *is* working?

What *is* moving in a positive direction?

Celebrate the smallest movements in the direction of progress!

....

....

....

....

....

My work makes me less angry (about the injustices in the world) because I feel every day I'm being a part of the solution rather than the problem. That feels good to me, even if there's always more I can be doing. I see my journey as a constant work in progress. (Lara Sheldrake)

'But it's moving so slowly!'

I hear you. The pace of change can feel very, very slow at times. When I've learned something or seen something for the first time, I can often find myself super-impatient, why don't they get it too?! Why can't they move faster!

I have to dig deep into compassion for others' journeys (with a different start-point and pace to mine), extending grace for others to learn (as I too am learning) and allowing the time and pace at which others choose to move. And yes, I do nudge!

REFLECTION POINT

Where is there *some* energy?

Who *is* moving?

Where can you join forces with others?

How can you sustain yourself as you engage with others who're moving at a slower pace than you?

....

....

....

....

....

And this is important – there's a difference between people learning at their own pace and investing time into that, and nothing moving because no-one is learning and changing. If it's the former, stay hopeful, keep nudging, keep sharing resources to support others in their learning and experimenting. If it's the latter, read on!

'Change takes time'

Yes, but not in a 'we'll just carry on as we've always done, because it will take time, take the foot off the gas, back off and leave it to someone else' kind of way! But in a 'let's make changes and start *now*', and with consistent, persistent small action, these small shifts will contribute to bigger changes over time. The change you wish to see will happen with small consistent action. Making the effort to pronounce a colleague's name correctly, including a new staff member in your conversation to enable them to feel welcome, crediting a more junior colleague for their work, using colleagues' preferred pronouns.[11] These are all examples of small behaviours that help create psychological safety. If you do them with your team, you positively shape your team's culture; if everyone does them consistently, you start to shift the organizational culture.

> Not everyone shares the same values and it's difficult to bring people on the journey. Resources are not focused on areas I'd like to work on so there's always a tension and challenge to highlight and advocate to progress things. I just keep challenging outdated thinking. I keep putting forward proposals and arguments that are well researched or evidence based. I build personal relationships and trust. (Ruth Lin Wong Holmes)

'Why don't they see it? Why are they resisting, why won't they change?'

Maybe they do see it, maybe they don't. Dr Kate Simpson reminds us that the status quo serves someone. Sometimes in our EDI change making we share the data, we allow the revealing, we nudge and continue to share resources to support the shifts. We gauge the level of energy required from us, and if there's still continued resistance, we may choose to walk away.

REFLECTION POINT

Who's the status quo serving?

How can what you are proposing meet their needs?

What's in it for them?

What's the area you want to influence – is it worth the energy?

....

....

....

....

....

'But I'm just one person! It's pointless me doing anything'

I notice clients will often ask me what's happening and what's improving in inclusion work more generally, across their sector, across other sectors. That's fine, I'm happy to share what progress I'm seeing and it can be encouraging and galvanizing to look at good practice. But this comment can also often come from a place of 'it's not really worth me doing anything unless I can see some immediate improvement'. There's an impatience for a quick fix for it to be 'worth it' or I'll do nothing. This person needs to connect with the 'why' of the change, see WIIFM (what's in it for me) and experience that even a small effort can start to shape the culture.

If you're the one feeling alone or like your efforts are a small drop in the ocean, I want to encourage you that your change-making action is worth doing! Yes, sometimes we need to regroup and re-strategize, often and regularly we'll need to rest and connect with others for a boost of support (use the following reflection point). Take the time you need for these strategies to energize you (see Chapter 3). But don't give up!

REFLECTION POINT

Who else is working on your issues or in your space?

Who can you connect with for a boost of inspiration, accountability and support?

....

....

....

....

....

I need to remind myself that I'm part of something. That my contribution may be tiny, but that there are millions of change makers around the world making tiny (and substantial) contributions. Ranting to friends with shared world views helps. As does meditating, really stopping and looking at my kids, caring for my plants. (Keri Jarvis)

'But I'm tired'

I hear you. Your change-making work can be exhausting. I love Banksy's reminder that when we're tired we can learn to rest rather than quit.

Go back to Chapter 3 and look at what needs to be topped up on your resilience map. Dig into your power practices, prioritize your rest, seek out your joy. Go back to Chapter 7 and invest in your ecosystem of support and accountability. Use the reflection point below to consider how to cope with future adversity.

Support looks like having regular touchpoints with those fellow alchemists where I don't have to explain myself, it looks like surrounding myself with expressions that feed my soul – art, music, dance. (Di Murray)

Being a relentless optimist helps me, and surrounding myself with people who also see the bright side. Looking after my mental and physical health, practising self-compassion, reflecting on the positives/gratitude, having a growth mindset/always seeking out the learnings I can get from every situation (positive and negative). Health habits I've always prioritized do pay off – and sometimes it's ok to 'down-shift' your life and do less. Your weekends don't have to be back-to-back to feel fulfilled; human connection is more important. (Fiona Young)

REFLECTION POINT

Knowing what you know now about your resilience (Chapter 3) and your ecosystem (Chapter 7), reflect and identify activities that you can take to sustain yourself through challenging times in the future.

How can you re-energize yourself today?

What permission can you give yourself for joy, fun, play and pleasure this weekend?

....
....
....
....
....

Choosing a growth mindset: Are you taking on too much responsibility?

In Chapter 1 we looked at what we can control (our habits, behaviours, what we do, what we say, and to some extent what we think and feel). What we can influence around us as change makers, through our actions, through what we role model, through having conversations and asking others to change.

That's it! You don't control anyone else, you can't make someone feel something, or do something. You're not responsible for others' feelings nor others' behaviours. You're responsible for your actions and responses, which others may choose to be influenced by.

When we're clear-sighted about this, it's powerful for our change making. We no longer have to take on more than we need to, or have capacity for. We can hold clearer boundaries with others. We can act with compassion and integrity, without over-committing and building up resentment. We can step up in our leadership without burning out.

We each have our own change-making role. Let's get super-clear what we can take responsibility for, and what we are doing to chip away at the wall, alongside others.

Dialling up your change-making brilliance!

We've explored how we sustain our own resilience while we navigate systems and are part of bringing about change. These summarizing principles help me when my hope-o-meter can get low, helping me step up without burning out:

1 **Intentionality.** Get to know yourself even better, your desires, your yes, your why. Allow yourself grace to change and grow over time, through your seasons and stages of life.
2 **Self-compassion.** Stay hopeful and compassionate, holding grace for your own and others' learning journeys.
3 **Progress not perfection.** Start small and imperfectly; continuing pragmatically is better than holding on to the perfect ideal that stays in your head and doing *nothing*. Focus on your small, small wins. Celebrate your progress.

4 **Seek out stories and lived experiences** that blow your mind because they're so different from yours. Break out of your echo chamber. Find your points of empathy and connection – you're extending your capacity to hold space for others.

5 **What to do with a wobble.** It's human and normal to have wobbles. Know that you *will* mess up. Dig into your growth mindset and celebrate your learning. Lean on your ecosystem. Stay shame free.

6 **Invest in your rest.** Prioritize staying refreshed and energized. Take a break rather than quit.

7 **Reconnect with your anger, your grief, your passion, your curiosity** – these drivers are fuel for your fire!

8 **Do more of what you love.** It's energizing and restorative to relish more joy, fun, wonder, creativity and pleasure in your day-to-day life.

9 **Find your sisterhood.** Seek out solidarity. Invest in your ecosystem of support and accountability.

10 **Keep showing up.** Give yourself permission! Keep going!

What I hope is on the horizon for change makers and your sustainability

There's a new world of doing work and life, and we can all choose to be part of it.

Together we can dismantle systems that hold us and others back. Together we can co-create new spaces that work for us and those around us, that respect the dignity and value of each human, and that cares for the earth.

It's not yet fully clear to me what this new world of work (and other spaces in society) look like. It's emerging,

As change makers now and of the future, we'll need to be re-birthing and re-creating systems.

We can start small, we can start in our own bodies and in our own unlearning.

This new way honours that our lives are interconnected, that my healing is connected to yours, that none of us are truly free until we're all free. This new way centres collective healing, collective liberation. This new way allows us to be in our bodies, calming our central nervous systems, connected to our breath, feeling our emotions, honouring our desires. This new way centres our healing and wellbeing. This new way centres justice, our humanity and the health of the earth.

I am here for it.

Unwind rewind: chapter summary

In Chapter 8 we've pulled together all the threads to support you to step up in your change-making leadership, without burning out.

We've built on the self-awareness, leadership and resilience foundations from Chapters I, 2 and 3, the full-body yes and make-it-happen practicality of Chapters 4 and 5, the systems awareness we unpacked in Chapter 6 and the shine-brighter focus from Chapter 7.

We've discussed how you can influence change and be part of dismantling systems at individual, team and systems levels. We've mapped your stakeholders, and looked at options if you don't feel you've access to the spaces of power. We've talked about how we can be part of co-creating new systems. You've got your hope-o-meter handy to support you to stay compassionate and keep your momentum going as change makers for the long haul.

Thank you for journeying with me through this book!

You've centred your wellbeing, you've learned power practices to integrate into your daily life, which will build your resilience and sustainability.

You've connected with your inner knowing, your full-body 'yes', your joy.

You've got clarity on your change-making purpose, your focus, you've found light-touch ways to stay on track with your own version of success, the life you want to create and the contribution you want to be making.

We've identified how systems oppress us, the barriers that exist, we've learned how we've colluded, and how we can unlearn. We've explored how we navigate, how we use our privilege as a superpower, to dismantle and co-create new spaces.

You've identified how you can supercharge your ecosystem of relationships, building collaboration and sisterhood.

We've done both the inner work and the outer work, we see how they're interconnected, and we want to be sustainable in both. You've identified your insights, takeaways and practical next steps to use your wisdom!

You can find all the power practices descriptors, exercises, and downloadable reusable templates at the book bonus section of my site.

Throughout this book we've talked about some meaty and intricate aspects of being human! I've invited you to go deep in your reflections, your inner work, and to step up in your outer work. Do seek specialist help with a coach to unpack further, and/or a clinician or therapist to support you with any trauma that's surfaced for you.

You're stepping up without burning out.

You are awesome! I trust you now feel powered up and inspired to take your next steps.

UNWIND REWIND

What's most important for you from this chapter?

What will you experiment with?

YOUR CHANGE-MAKER PROGRESS + ACTION TRACKER

- This is what I'm experimenting with (the action I'm taking to make a difference).

- This is what I'm noticing.

AFFIRMATIONS

'I am stepping up.'

'I am centring liberation, healing and solidarity.'

'I'm dismantling systems that no longer serve us.'

'There is room for all of us.'

'I'm unlearning the old ways.'

'I'm experimenting with new ways.'

Notes

Introduction

1 Watson, Lilla (2004) Keynote address: A contribution to change: cooperation out of conflict conference: celebrating difference, embracing equality, Aboriginal Activists Group Queensland 1970s, Hobart, 21–24 September

2 Intergovernmental Panel on Climate Change (2021) AR6 climate change 2021: The physical science basis, www.ipcc.ch/report/ar6/wg1/ (archived at https://perma.cc/P6XX-YLHR)

3 Adapted from Brown, B (2017) *Braving the wilderness*, brenebrown. com/blog/2018/05/17/dehumanizing-always-starts-with-language/ (archived at https://perma.cc/M2UZ-EVJE)

4 Diels, K (2017) Jan Mcneil, Stand Up to 2017, http://www.jacmcneil. com/wp-content/uploads/2017/01/STAND-UP-TO-2017-Final-1.pdf (archived at https://perma.cc/P6A2-2DTM)

5 McKinsey (2021) Women in the workplace 2021, www.mckinsey.com/ featured-insights/diversity-and-inclusion/women-in-the-workplace (archived at https://perma.cc/V7KN-A7Q4)

6 Deloitte (2021) Women @ work: A global outlook, www2.deloitte.com/ content/dam/Deloitte/global/Documents/About-Deloitte/gx-women-at-work-global-outlook-report.pdf (archived at https://perma.cc/3JB2-Y3GK)

7 Pinkus, E (2021) CNBC|SurveyMonkey poll: International Women's Day 2021, Curiosity at Work, www.surveymonkey.com/curiosity/ cnbc-women-at-work-2021/ (archived at https://perma.cc/DMC6-CF33)

8   McKinsey (2021) Women in the workplace 2021, www.mckinsey.com/
    featured-insights/diversity-and-inclusion/women-in-the-workplace
    (archived at https://perma.cc/V7KN-A7Q4)

9   Box, G and Draper, N (1987) *Empirical model-building and response
    surfaces*, Wiley, New York

10 Korzybski, A (1933) *Science and sanity: An introduction to non-
    Aristotelian systems and general semantics*, Institute of General
    Semantics, Englewood, NJ

11 Tolle, E, (2016) *The power of now: A guide to spiritual enlightenment*,
    Hodder & Stoughton, London

12 Criado Perez, C (2019) *Invisible women: Exposing data bias in a world
    designed for men*, Abrams Press, New York City

13 Clemmons, J (2020) Black families have inherited trauma, but we can
    change that, Healthline, 26 August, www.healthline.com/health/
    parenting/epigenetics-and-the-black-experience#Our-ancestors-trauma-
    lives-on (archived at https://perma.cc/383P-JMFN)

Chapter 1

1   Gilbert, P (2009) *The compassionate mind*, Constable, London

2   Cowen, A S and Keltner, D (2017), Abstract, 19 September, www.pnas.
    org/content/114/38/E7900.abstract (archived at https://perma.cc/
    QVN4-ZKHR); Amina Khan at *LA Times*, What is love actually? The
    world's languages describe emotions very differently, www.latimes.com/
    science/story/2019-12-19/emotions-universal-languages-differ (archived
    at https://perma.cc/36R5-LP85); Lindquist, K A (2019), *Science*, 20
    December, www.science.org/doi/full/10.1126/science.aaw8160 (archived
    at https://perma.cc/P5L2-MDXE)

3   Patel, J and Patel, P (2019) Consequences of repression of emotion:
    Physical health, mental health and general wellbeing, *International
    Journal of Psychotherapy Practice and Research* **1** (3), February,
    openaccesspub.org/ijpr/article/999 (archived at https://perma.cc/
    JM75-TWYZ)

4   Van der Kolk, B (2014) *The body keeps the score: Mind, brain and
    body in the transformation of trauma*, Viking, New York City

5 David, S (2016) *Emotional agility: Get unstuck, embrace change, thrive in work and life*, Avery, New York City

6 Gruman, J, Schneider, F and Coutts, L (2016) (eds) *Applied social psychology: Understanding and addressing social and practical problems*, Sage Publications, Thousand Oaks, CA

7 Taylor, J (2009) *My stroke of insight: A brain scientist's personal journey*, Penguin, New York City

8 Leading Effectively (2020) How to banish stress and burnout by stopping rumination, Center for Creative Leadership, 16 November, www.ccl.org/articles/leading-effectively-articles/banish-stress-stop-ruminating/ (archived at https://perma.cc/28Y6-UZCB)

9 Rock, D (2009) Managing with the brain in mind, *Strategy+Business* (56), 2uxlo5u7jf11pm3f36oan8d6-wpengine.netdna-ssl.com/wp-content/uploads/2016/06/ManagingWBrainInMind.pdf (archived at https://perma.cc/AX3E-NDFP)

10 Vaish, A, Grossmann, T and Woodward, A (2008) Not all emotions are created equal: the negativity bias in social-emotional development, *Psychological Bulletin,* **134** (3), pp 383, www.ncbi.nlm.nih.gov/pmc/articles/PMC3652533/ (archived at https://perma.cc/7QBY-93XT)

11 Burns, D (1999) *Feeling good: The new mood therapy*, HarperCollins, New York City

12 McGreevey, S (2015) Relaxation response prives positive, *The Harvard Gazette,*13 October, news.harvard.edu/gazette/story/2015/10/relaxation-response-proves-positive/ (archived at https://perma.cc/LSQ6-WZEA)

13 Denning, S (2018) The benefits of meditation in business, Forbes, 2 February, www.forbes.com/sites/stephaniedenning/2018/02/02/the-benefits-of-meditation-in-business/?sh=5f79179654f5 (archived at https://perma.cc/T76A-J2MP)

14 Mitchell, M (2013) Dr Herbert Benson's Relaxation Response, March 29, www.psychologytoday.com/us/blog/heart-and-soul-healing/201303/dr-herbert-benson-s-relaxation-response (archived at https://perma.cc/N2FH-TLYC)

15 Chopra, D (2013) Collective flow state: From the who to your team, Deepak Chopra, 8 February, www.deepakchopra.com/articles/collective-flow-state-from-the-who-to-your-team/ (archived at https://perma.cc/BN9N-HKCU)

Chapter 2

1 Jean-Baptiste, A (2020) Making inclusive design a priority, Porchlight, www.porchlightbooks.com/blog/changethis/2020/making-inclusive-design-a-priority (archived at https://perma.cc/333J-BHTE)

2 Dweck, C (2012) *Mindset: Changing the way you think to fulfil your potential*, Ballantine Books, New York City

3 Dweck, C (2014) The power of yet, TED Talk, 12 September, www.youtube.com/watch?v=J-swZaKN2Ic (archived at https://perma.cc/599M-EPVY)

4 Murray, K and Smith, F (2018) Working woman's guide to... befriending your inner critic, Collective Catalyst, 29 January, www.catalyst-collective.com/blog/inner-critic (archived at https://perma.cc/9MCZ-852W)

5 Mohr, T (2014) *Playing big: Find your voice, your vision and make things happen*, Hutchinson, New York City

6 Johnson, W, and Mohr, T (2013) Women need to realize work isn't school, *Harvard Business Review*, 11 January, hbr.org/2013/01/women-need-to-realize-work-isnt-schol (archived at https://perma.cc/32QQ-86NH)

7 Leading Effectively (2020) How to banish stress and burnout by stopping rumination, Center for Creative Leadership, 16 November, www.ccl.org/articles/leading-effectively-articles/banish-stress-stop-ruminating/ (archived at https://perma.cc/28Y6-UZCB)

8 Crenshaw, K (1996) *Critical race theory: The key writings that formed the movement*, The New Press, New York City

9 Collins, P (2008) *Black feminist thought: Knowledge consciousness and the politics of empowerment*, Routledge Classics, Abingdon

10 Batliwala, S (2013) *Engaging with empowerment: An intellectual and experiential journey*, Women Unlimited; Batliwala, S (2019) *All about power: Understanding social power and power structures*, CREA

11 Lean In (2021) Working at the intersection: What Black women are up against, leanin.org/black-women-racism-discrimination-at-work (archived at https://perma.cc/TY9L-G495)

12 Vitti, A (2014) *Woman code: Perfect your cycle, amplify your fertility, supercharge your sex drive and become a power source*, HarperOne, New York City

Chapter 3

1 McKinsey and Lean In (2021) Women at work 2021, wiw-report. s3.amazonaws.com/Women_in_the_Workplace_2021.pdf (archived at https://perma.cc/65HH-VBEC)

2 Thaler, R and Sunstein, C (2008) *Nudge: Improving decisions about health, wealth, and happiness*, Yale University Press, New Haven, CT

3 Lucy Sheridan during *Inevitable* training programme

4 Rohr, R (2009) *The naked now: Learning to see as the mystics see*, The Crossroad Publishing Company, New York City

5 www.katycatalyst.com/change-makers-book (archived at https://perma.cc/N3N4-TDG6)

6 The Nap Ministry (2021), How will you be useless to capitalism today? 3 August, thenapministry.wordpress.com (archived at https://perma.cc/M37J-864F)

7 Shkodzik, K (2020) How to plan your work around your period, *Flo Health*, 14 May, flo.health/menstrual-cycle/health/period/plan-work-around-your-period (archived at https://perma.cc/DKE9-8R82)

8 Kondo, M (2014) *The life-changing magic of tidying: A simple, effective way to banish clutter forever*, Vermilion, London

9 LLeras, A and Ariga, A (2011) Brief and rare mental 'breaks' keep you focused: Deactivation and reactivation of task goals preempt vigilance decrements, *Cognition,* 118 (3), pp 439–43, www.researchgate.net/publication/222820913_Brief_and_rare_mental_breaks_keep_you_focused_Deactivation_and_reactivation_of_task_goals_preempt_vigilance_decrements (archived at https://perma.cc/T5BR-WVJN)

10 Globokar, L (2020) The power of visualization and how to use it, *Forbes*, 5 March, www.forbes.com/sites/lidijaglobokar/2020/03/05/the-power-of-visualization-and-how-to-use-it/?sh=7f8e5c2c6497 (archived at https://perma.cc/PB3T-AVXD)

11 www.katycatalyst.com/change-makers-book (archived at https://perma.cc/CF2K-V6F5)

12 Vanbuskirk, S (2021) The mental health benefits of making your bed, Verywell Mind, 29 January, www.verywellmind.com/mental-health-benefits-of-making-your-bed-5093540 (archived at https://perma.cc/4GMK-7T8B)

Chapter 4

1 Bhasin, M (2017) *The authenticity principle: Resist conformity, embrace differences, and transform how you live, work, and lead*, Melanin Made Press, Toronto

2 Mohr, T (2014) *Playing big: Find your voice, your vision and make things happen*, Penguin, New York City

3 Maderer, J (2020) Women interrupted: A new strategy for male-dominated discussions, Carnegie Mellon University, 21 October, www.cmu.edu/news/stories/archives/2020/october/women-interrupted-debate.html (archived at https://perma.cc/RR2C-3EX9)

4 Seligman, M (2017) *Authentic happiness: Using the new positive psychology to realize your potential for lasting fulfillment*, Nicholas Brealey, London

5 Brown, A (2019) *Pleasure activism: The politics of feeling good*, AK Press, Chico

6 Diagram created by author and psychological astrologer Andres Zuzunaga in 2011, first appearing in Vilaseca, B (2012) *Qué harías si no tuvieras miedo*, Connecta, Barcelona

7 Hendricks, G (2009) *The big leap: Conquer your hidden fear and take life to the next level*, HarperCollins, New York City

8 Sheridan, L (2021) Inevitable training programme, www.proofcoaching.com/inevitable (archived at https://perma.cc/54KT-L7MG)

Chapter 5

1 Murashev, N (2011) Why luck has nothing to do with it, *Forbes*, 8 November, www.forbes.com/sites/lesliebradshaw/2011/11/08/why-luck-has-nothing-to-do-with-it/?sh=26c6efbb4f98 (archived at https://perma.cc/A5AY-HFHV)

2 Thomashauer, R (2016) *Pussy: A reclamation*, Hay House, Carlsbad

3 Seligman, M (2017) *Authentic happiness: Using the new positive psychology to realize your potential for lasting fulfilment*, Nicholas Brealey, London

4   Kelly, J (2021) Indeed Study shows that worker burnout is at frightening high levels: Here is what you need to do now, *Forbes*, 5 April, www.forbes.com/sites/jackkelly/2021/04/05/indeed-study-shows-that-worker-burnout-is-at-frighteningly-high-levels-here-is-what-you-need-to-do-now/?sh=641c639123bb (archived at https://perma.cc/AJ94-CLMM)

5   Csíkszentmihályi, M (2008) *Flow: The psychology of optimal experience*, Harper Perennial, New York City

6   Kotler, S (2019) Create a work environment that fosters flow, *Harvard Business Review*, 6 May, hbr.org/2014/05/create-a-work-environment-that-fosters-flow (archived at https://perma.cc/7PDX-RZ3E)

7   Clear, J (2018) *Atomic habits: An easy & proven way to build good habits & break bad ones*, Random House, New York City

8   Robinson, B (2021) The surprising benefits of 'microbreaks' for engagement, productivity and career success, *Forbes,* 28 March, www.forbes.com/sites/bryanrobinson/2021/03/28/the-surprising-benefits-of-microbreaks-for-engagement-productivity-and-career-success/?sh=55f00a277150 (archived at https://perma.cc/4MCG-P8L5)

9   Armstrong, C (2018) *The mother of all jobs: How to have children and a career and stay sane(ish),* Green Tree, London

10 Silva, C, Carter, N M and Beninger, A (2012) Good intentions, imperfect execution? Women get fewer of the "hot jobs" needed to advance, www.catalyst.org/wp-content/uploads/2019/01/Good_Intentions_Imperfect_Execution_Women_Get_Fewer_of_the_Hot_Jobs_Needed_to_Advance.pdf (archived at https://perma.cc/5989-43FX); Correll, S J and Mackenzie, L N (2016) To succeed in tech, women need more visibility, *Harvard Business Review*, 13 September, hbr.org/2016/09/to-succeed-in-tech-women-need-more-visibility (archived at https://perma.cc/4GC5-K8UK); Babcock, L, Recalde, M P and Vesterlund, L (2018) Why women volunteer for tasks that don't lead to promotions, *Harvard Business Review*, 16 July, hbr.org/2018/07/why-women-volunteer-for-tasks-that-dont-lead-to-promotions (archived at https://perma.cc/CW4V-3PTL)

11 Febos, M (2017) Do you want to be known for your writing, or for your swift email responses?, *Catapult Magazine*, 23 March, catapult.co/stories/do-you-want-to-be-known-for-your-writing-or-for-your-swift-email-responses (archived at https://perma.cc/RHQ2-UF34)

12 Daminger, A (2019) The cognitive dimension of household labor, *American Sociological Review,* **84** (4), pp 609–33, journals.sagepub. com/doi/10.1177/0003122419859007 (archived at https://perma. cc/5BJS-5WSQ)

Chapter 6

1 Hegde, S (2019) What is internalized oppression?, *Science ABC*, 13 November, www.scienceabc.com/social-science/what-is-internalized-oppression-definition-h3h3-example.html (archived at https://perma.cc/ Y4T7-2EV3)

2 Etomi, O (2017) As women, we're taught to police other women – here's why, Huffpost, 24 March, www.huffpost.com/entry/women-policing-women-the-prison-of-belief_b_58d4f098e4b06c3d3d3e6c7e (archived at https://perma.cc/W6YN-KGAZ)

3 National Museum of African American History & Culture (2021) Social identities and systems of oppression, nmaahc.si.edu/learn/ talking-about-race/topics/social-identities-and-systems-oppression (archived at https://perma.cc/N3KZ-XJ93)

4 Armstrong, J and Ghaboos, J (2019) Gender bias in workplace culture curbs careers, Murray Edwards College, University of Cambridge, www.murrayedwards.cam.ac.uk/sites/default/files/files/CWM%20 Gender%20Bias%20REPORT%20FINAL%2020190211.pdf (archived at https://perma.cc/B2FB-RVQ2)

5 Crossley, A (2015) Women leaders: does likeability really matter? Stanford, 24 June, gender.stanford.edu/news-publications/gender-news/ women-leaders-does-likeability-really-matter (archived at https://perma. cc/C3T6-C4YC); leanin.org/education/what-is-likeability-bias (archived at https://perma.cc/C94M-9KTM)

6 Asare, J (2019) Overcoming the angry Black woman stereotype, *Forbes*, 31 May, www.forbes.com/sites/janicegassam/2019/05/31/overcoming-the-angry-black-woman-stereotype/?sh=5199a02b1fce (archived at https://perma.cc/2PWJ-JFZ6)

7 Byng, R (2017) Failure is not an option: the pressure Black women feel to succeed, *Forbes*, 31 August, www.forbes.com/sites/rhoneshabyng/2017/08/31/failure-is-not-an-option-the-pressure-black-women-feel-to-succeed/?sh=7958919b3fad (archived at https://perma.cc/5ZKZ-5P63)

8 Eddo-Lodge, R (2018) *Why I'm no longer talking to white people about race*, Bloomsbury, London

9 Hewlett, S, Rashid, R, and Sherbin, L (2020) Disrupt bias drive value, Coqual, coqual.org/wp-content/uploads/2020/09/CoqualDisruptBiasDriveValue090720.pdf (archived at https://perma.cc/H2MN-U35X)

10 Hunt, V, Layton, D and Prince, S (2015) Why diversity matters, McKinsey, 1 January, www.mckinsey.com/business-functions/people-and-organizational-performance/our-insights/why-diversity-matters (archived at https://perma.cc/66AP-UELK)

11 Edmondson, A (2014) Building a psychologically safe workplace, TEDx Talks [YouTube], 5 May, www.youtube.com/watch?v=LhoLuui9gX8 (archived at https://perma.cc/Y26K-XAGY)

12 Mindgym (2021) How to build inclusive leadership at work, uk.themindgym.com/resources/how-to-build-inclusive-leadership-at-work/ (archived at https://perma.cc/2YYD-N4SS)

13 Yoon, H (2020) How to respond to microaggressions, *The New York Times*, 3 March, www.nytimes.com/2020/03/03/smarter-living/how-to-respond-to-microaggressions.html (archived at https://perma.cc/HD6E-E733)

14 Craddock, K (2021) 'It's not in our head'... and yet pain is in our brain, Embrace Race, www.embracerace.org/resources/its-not-in-our-head-and-yet-pain-is-in-our-brain-why-racialized-exclusion-hurts-and-how-we-can-remain-resilient (archived at https://perma.cc/4334-WBEJ)

15 Smith, K (2019) There's nothing 'micro' about the impact of microaggressions, PCOM, 12 August, www.pcom.edu/about/departments/marketing-and-communications/digest-magazine/digest-featured-stories/theres-nothing-micro-about-the-impact-of-microaggressions.html (archived at https://perma.cc/RX7E-LWT4)

16 Gilovich, T (2017) The headwinds/tailwinds asymmetry [YouTube], www.youtube.com/watch?v=xXoe64Er6z0 (archived at https://perma.cc/25XF-Q6UU)

17 Malacrino, D (2020) How the rich get richer, IMF, 30 November, blogs. imf.org/2020/11/30/how-the-rich-get-richer/ (archived at https://perma. cc/VL82-64EX)

18 Bendixen, S (2020) Women leaders and luck, Center for Creative Leadership, 20 November, www.ccl.org/articles/leading-effectively-articles/women-luck-credit-success/ (archived at https://perma. cc/3727-3LQT)

19 Nixon, S (2019) The coin model of privilege and critical allyship: implications for health, BMC Public Health, bmcpublichealth. biomedcentral.com/track/pdf/10.1186/s12889-019-7884-9.pdf (archived at https://perma.cc/7BNS-LBQA)

20 Vinnicombe, S et al (2021) The female FTSE board report, Cranfield School of Management, www.cranfield.ac.uk/som/research-centres/gender-leadership-and-inclusion-centre/female-ftse-board-report (archived at https://perma.cc/49JZ-99RM)

21 FTSE Women Leaders (2021), Hampton-Alexander Review 2021, ftsewomenleaders.com/wp-content/uploads/2021/03/Hampton-Alexander-Review-Report-2020_web.pdf (archived at https://perma.cc/CXL6-7GMF)

22 Carrick, A (2021) More UK funds run by men called Dave than women, City AM, 8 March, www.cityam.com/more-uk-funds-run-by-men-called-dave-than-women/ (archived at https://perma.cc/3DWJ-LTBB)

23 World Economic Forum (2021) Global gender gap report 2021, World Economic Forum, 31 March, www.weforum.org/reports/ab6795a1-960c-42b2-b3d5-587eccda6023 (archived at https://perma.cc/3R8J-URXS)

24 Evans, T (2020) Ethnicity pay gaps, Office for National Statistics, 12 October, www.ons.gov.uk/employmentandlabourmarket/peopleinwork/earningsandworkinghours/articles/ethnicitypaygapsingreatbritain/2019 (archived at https://perma.cc/58LT-YTWP)

25 Tortoise (2021) The Tortoise Disability 100 Report, Tortoise, www. tortoisemedia.com/disability100-report/ (archived at https://perma.cc/YM2S-JMBQ)

26 Stonewall (2018) LGBT in Britain – Work Report, 25 April, www. stonewall.org.uk/lgbt-britain-work-report (archived at https://perma. cc/9H7C-N6UJ)

27 McKinsey and Lean In (2021) Women in the Workplace 2021, wiw-report.s3.amazonaws.com/Women_in_the_Workplace_2021.pdf (archived at https://perma.cc/65HH-VBEC)

28 Tulshyan, R (2020) The problem isn't men, it's patriarchy. The problem isn't white people, it's white supremacy. The problem isn't straight people, it's homophobia. Recognize systems of oppression before letting individual defensiveness paralyze you from dismantling them. [Twitter] 24 June, www.facebook.com/yourprivilegeisshowing/photos/httpstwitte rcomrtulshyanstatus1275813568177291264s21i-say-this-in-my-classesthe-/2673421456313511/ (archived at https://perma.cc/3QTA-XQXD)

29 Martin, G (2021) No, not all men. But too many. [Instagram], 11 March, www.instagram.com/tv/CMR9iKBHAZc/ (archived at https://perma.cc/J2L4-DZQ3)

30 Reid, N (2021) Not all men. Not all white people. It's so goddamn draining and nothing but a deflection from addressing the issue. We'd be so much further in society if people were less interested in image perception and actually tackling the issue at hand. [Instagram] 12 March, www.instagram.com/p/CMT6DswFLjB/ (archived at https://perma.cc/Z7CH-68VZ)

31 Gerstandt , J (2011) Inclusion is activist, Joe Gerstandt, 16 May, www.joegerstandt.com/2011/05/inclusion-is-activist/ (archived at https://perma.cc/R8J5-AM6U)

32 Jackson, C (2020) Catrice M. Jackson: 'If you don't have an anti-racism plan, you plan to *be* racist', *Harper's Bazaar*, 8 June, www.harpersbazaar.com/uk/culture/a32781443/catrice-jackson-anti-racism-action/ (archived at https://perma.cc/FT46-YHLK); Jackson, C (2017) *White spaces missing faces: Why women of color don't trust white women*, Catriceology Enterprises

33 DePino, M and Saahene M (2018) From privilege to progress, fromprivilegetoprogress.org (archived at https://perma.cc/X66L-RHHK)

34 DiAngelo, R (2018) *White fragility: Why it's so hard for white people to talk about racism*, Beacon Press; Saad, L F and DiAngelo, R (2020) *Me and white supremacy: How to recognise your privilege, combat racism and change the world*, Quercus

35 Cargle, R (2018) When feminism is white supremacy in heels, *Harper's Bazaar*, 16 August, www.harpersbazaar.com/culture/politics/a22717725/what-is-toxic-white-feminism/ (archived at https://perma.cc/HX8Q-YRDU)

36 Myers, V (2021) Owning her truth: Fevi's story, Verna Myers Company, 28 September, www.vernamyers.com/2021/09/28/owning-her-truth-fevis-story/ (archived at https://perma.cc/4SGT-SMLP)

37 Murphy, C (2020) What is white savior complex, and why is it harmful? Here's what experts say, Health.com, 20 September, www.health.com/mind-body/health-diversity-inclusion/white-savior-complex (archived at https://perma.cc/RB66-5PPP)

38 Mohr, T and Johnson, W (2013) Women need to realize work is not school, Harvard Business Review, 11 January, hbr.org/2013/01/women-need-to-realize-work-isnt-schol (archived at https://perma.cc/32QQ-86NH)

39 Dabiri, E (2021) *What white people can do next: From allyship to coalition*, Penguin, London

40 Craddock, K (2021) 'It's not in our head'... and yet pain is in our brain, Embrace Race, www.embracerace.org/resources/its-not-in-our-head-and-yet-pain-is-in-our-brain-why-racialized-exclusion-hurts-and-how-we-can-remain-resilient (archived at https://perma.cc/4334-WBEJ)

Chapter 7

1 Poehler, A (2011) Harvard University 2011 Class day speech by Amy Poehler [Youtube], www.youtube.com/watch?v=7WvdxgGpNVU&t=4s (archived at https://perma.cc/U2CP-L8JH)

2 Ibarra, H (2019) A lack of sponsorship is keeping women from advancing into leadership, *Harvard Business Review*, 19 August, hbr.org/2019/08/a-lack-of-sponsorship-is-keeping-women-from-advancing-into-leadership (archived at https://perma.cc/ZPN2-WNUS)

3 Hendricks, G (2009) *The big leap: Conquer your hidden fear and take life to the next level*, HarperOne, New York City

4 Pazzanese, C (2020) Women less inclined to self-promote than men, even for a job, *Harvard Gazette*, news.harvard.edu/gazette/story/2020/02/men-better-than-women-at-self-promotion-on-job-leading-to-inequities/ (archived at https://perma.cc/6SXN-VMW3); Kasanoff, B (2016) 40 ways to self-promote without being a jerk, 11 July, *Forbes*, www.forbes.com/sites/brucekasanoff/2016/07/11/40-ways-to-self-promote-without-being-a-jerk/?sh=1e36d4656851 (archived at https://perma.cc/5363-9S89)

5 Chira, S (2017) The universal phenomenon of men interrupting women, *The New York Times*, 14 June, www.nytimes.com/2017/06/14/business/women-sexism-work-huffington-kamala-harris.html (archived at https://perma.cc/WD36-QMYB)

6 The Guardian (2021) The authority gap: why women still aren't taken seriously, Mary Ann Sieghart [Podcast], podcasts.podinstall.com/guardian-today-focus/202107260200-authority-gap-why-women-still-arent-taken-seriously.html (archived at https://perma.cc/9ABC-FZFX)

7 Tulshyan, R and Burey, J (2021) Stop telling women they have imposter syndrome, *Harvard Business Review*, 11 February, hbr.org/2021/02/stop-telling-women-they-have-imposter-syndrome (archived at https://perma.cc/NJ6Q-SYHJ)

8 Mukwashi, A (2020) *But where are you really from? On identity, humanhood and hope*, SPCK Publishing, London

9 The Conversation Podcast, BBC Sounds, *Women leading change in NGOs*, 25 October 2021, Amanda Khozi Mukwashi and Summer Nasser, www.bbc.co.uk/programmes/w3ct1p96 (archived at https://perma.cc/Z6DQ-L7SL)

10 Gupta, G (2016) The power of saying 'I don't know', *Forbes,* 29 November

11 Iyer, D (2021) The map: Social change ecosystem, http://deepaiyer.com/the-map-social-change-ecosystem/ (archived at https://perma.cc/D8DK-3YMQ)

12 Uzzi, B (2019) Research: Men and women need different kinds of networks to succeed, *Harvard Business Review,* 25 February, hbr.org/2019/02/research-men-and-women-need-different-kinds-of-networks-to-succeed (archived at https://perma.cc/2EQB-BV8P)

13 Ibarra, H (2016) Why strategic networking is harder for women, 4 July, herminiaibarra.com/why-strategic-networking-is-harder-for-women/ (archived at https://perma.cc/K6TA-XLXC)

14 Friedman, A and Sow, A (2019) Shine theory is a practice of mutual investment in each other, www.shinetheory.com (archived at https://perma.cc/9FHT-6CJC); Bastian, R (2019) The importance of network diversity, *Forbes*, 9 October, www.forbes.com/sites/rebekahbastian/2019/10/09/the-importance-of-network-diversity/?sh=58d5ef781df0 (archived at https://perma.cc/4JQS-N74E)

15 Watts, D (2003) *Six degrees: The science of a connected age*, Vintage, London

Chapter 8

1 Baldwin, J (1962) As much truth as one can bear, *The New York Times Book Review*, 14 January, *The New York Times*

2 Davis, A (2017) Revolution today [Video], Centre de Cultura Contemporania Barcelona, www.cccb.org/en/multimedia/videos/angela-davis/227656 (archived at https://perma.cc/F2UJ-8GV4)

3 4 News (2021) Miami's 'climate gentrification', The Four Cast podcast, 15 September, www.channel4.com/news/miamis-climate-gentrification (archived at https://perma.cc/Z9NB-DQWR)

4 Reay, C (2021) Why don't we have more disabled people on our staff? [Instagram], 19 August, www.instagram.com/p/CSwThyast8U (archived at https://perma.cc/CC7Z-42VL)

5 Fick-Cooper, L et al (2020) Confronting wicked problems: Reimagined leadership strategies for societal impact, Center for Creative Leadership, www.ccl.org/articles/white-papers/reimagined-leadership-strategies-for-nonprofits-the-social-sector/ (archived at https://perma.cc/9RQ9-UX76)

6 Wharton Business Daily (2020) Does pay transparency help close the gender wage gap? [Podcast], www.wharton.upenn.edu/story/does-pay-transparency-help-close-the-gender-wage-gap/ (archived at https://perma.cc/TZ48-ZYFL)

7 Bergdorf, M (2021) 3 October [Instagram], www.instagram.com/p/CUkOnlsgQeT/ (archived at https://perma.cc/ZJ6D-SRVS)

8 Zheng, L (2019) How to show white men that diversity and inclusion efforts need them, *Harvard Business Review*, 28 October, hbr. org/2019/10/how-to-show-white-men-that-diversity-and-inclusion-efforts-need-them (archived at https://perma.cc/LX9S-C6VW)

9 Janis, M (2017) The arc of history: How to bend towards justice?, Huffpost, 9 August, https://www.huffpost.com/entry/the-arc-of-history-how-to_b_11343402 (archived at https://perma.cc/U9J9-EE26)

10 The Liturgists Podcast (2014), *Spiral Dynamics*, episode 5, September, open.spotify.com/episode/3QkKFhaFSXvLgXkMj4Blbf (archived at https://perma.cc/6M7Q-6WPN)

11 What are personal pronouns and why do they matter?, www. mypronouns.org/what-and-why/ (archived at https://perma.cc/X7XP-XTVY)

Resources to complement
this book and
working with Katy

Y ou can find out more about Katy's coaching, change-maker programmes and business mastermind at www.katycatalyst.com. Further reading, a full list of affirmations, audio versions of the visualizations, downloadable bonuses including templates of all the power practices are available at www.katycatalyst.com/change-makers-book. Join Katy's list of subscribers to receive regular power practice top-ups and inspirational resources to support you as you step up without burning out!

Index